AMERICAN INDIAN MYTHOLOGY

Evelyn Wolfson

Enslow Publishers, Inc.

40 Industrial Road	PO Box 38
Box 398	Aldershot
Berkeley Heights, NJ 07922	Hants GU12 6BP
USA	UK

http://www.enslow.com

Acknowledgments

My sincere thanks and appreciation for their expert advice, criticism, comments, and permissions to: Basil Johnston, linguist and lecturer in the Department of Ethnology at the Royal Ontario Museum; Dr. Theda Perdue of the University of North Carolina; Doty Coyote; Elaine Dohan, Gladys McKinnon, and Dacia Callen.

Library of Congress Cataloging-in-Publication Data

Wolfson, Evelyn.
    American Indian mythology / Evelyn Wolfson.
       p. cm. — (Mythology)
    Includes bibliographical references and index.
    Summary: Discusses various American Indian myths, including creation stories and tales of principal characters.
    ISBN 0-7660-1411-8
    1. Indian mythology—North America—Juvenile literature. [1. Indians of North America—Folklore. 2. Folklore—North America.] I. Title. II. Mythology (Berkeley Heights, N.J.)
    E98.R3 W79 2000
    299'.72—dc21   00-028781

Printed in the United States of America

10 9 8 7 6 5 4 3 2

To Our Readers: We have done our best to make sure all Internet addresses in this book were active and appropriate when we went to press. However, the author and the publisher have no control over and assume no liability for the material available on those Internet sites or on other Web sites they may link to. Any comments or suggestions can be sent by e-mail to comments@enslow.com or to the address on the back cover.

Cover and Illustrations by: William Sauts Bock

✦✕ CONTENTS ✕✦

Preface   5

Culture Map of the
American Indians   6

1 *Raven Steals Daylight from the Sky*
Northwest (Tsimshians) 11

2 *The Moon Epic*
Coast Plateau (Salish) 24

3 *Tolowim-Woman and Butterfly-Man*
California (Maidu) 36

4 *How the World Was Made*
Southeast (Cherokees) 49

5 *Buffalo Husband*
Northern Plains (Blackfeet) 60

6 *Winter-Man's Fury*
Southern Plains (Cheyennes) 72

7 *The Kachinas Are Coming*
Southwest (Hopi) 84

8 *Mandamin*
Western Great Lakes (Anishinabes) 97

9 *Glooscap the Teacher*
Eastern Woodlands (Micmacs) 107

Glossary 119

Chapter Notes 121

Further Reading and Internet Addresses 124

Index 127

Titles in the Mythology series:

American Indian Mythology
ISBN 0-7660-1411-8

Celtic Mythology
ISBN 0-7660-1413-4

Chinese Mythology
ISBN 0-7660-1412-6

Egyptian Mythology
ISBN 0-7660-1407-X

*Gods and Goddesses
in Greek Mythology*
ISBN 0-7660-1408-8

Inuit Mythology
ISBN 0-7660-1559-9

Mayan and Aztec Mythology
ISBN 0-7660-1409-6

Roman Mythology
ISBN 0-7660-1558-0

PREFACE

American Indian myths and legends often include a variety of characters with supernatural powers, including animals and heavenly bodies, who help to shape the universe. Unlike the myths of Europe, Africa, and Asia, where the point of a story is often made to express a moral, these stories seldom moralize. However, they do tell stories that humanize the past.

In their early days, the Indians did not have a written language. Therefore, all myths were recorded by American ethnologists and anthropologists who relied on English-speaking Indian interpreters to translate for them. Most of these original translations contain only a skeleton of a story—only as much information as the storyteller was interested in conveying.

Eventually, many Indians learned to write in their own language and recorded stories in both their language and English. Still, there has never been a systematic method of collecting and/or recording American Indian myths in any of the Indian languages, and many of the stories remain scattered throughout the journals of American anthropologists. Most of the tales I include in this book are taken from these early sources.[1]

In my retelling, I have tried, as the Lenape say, to do so with a *thinking heart*. I stay as close to the original translations as possible, and I try to retain the spirit of the original, as if the old-time storytellers were speaking through me—even though I know the eye is less tolerant to words on a page than the ear is to a human voice.

Traditional American Indian tales rarely had a beginning, middle, or end. Storytellers could begin their

NASS R.

TSIMSHIANS

BLACKFEET

SALISH

CHEYENNES

MAIDU

Pacific
Ocean

HOPI

CULTURE MAP OF THE
AMERICAN INDIANS

ANISHINABES

MICMACS

Great Lakes

CHEROKEES

Atlantic Ocean

N
E
W
S

story wherever they chose because the tales were already so forcefully imprinted in the hearts and minds of the people. These stories were so real for them that a Blackfeet audience could feel the thunder of buffalo hoofs when they heard the story of how the buffalo gave themselves to the people. Likewise, Coast Salish tribes could hear the splash of the great migrating salmon when they listened to how Young Moon brought salmon to their rivers. People listened over and over again to their traditional stories, savoring the unique style and wit of each new storyteller.

Storytellers were always free to express their own individual interpretations of courage, cunning, and cowardice, as well as of pity and love. Thus, there are many versions of the same tale, even within a single culture area where people share a similar lifestyle. Rather than try to combine several versions of a story from one area, I have stayed faithful to a single version. For example, among tribes of the Pacific Northwest, who lived along the coast from northern California to southern Alaska, there are many versions of how Raven stole daylight. Only the Tsimshians' version is told here to avoid homogenizing the culture of the region. The original homeland of the Tsimshians now lies in northern British Columbia (Canada) and southern Alaska.[2]

A culture area is a geographical region occupied by people whose cultures are similar. For example, the lifestyles of the Tsimshians and Tlingits of the Northwest Coast are similar, but they are significantly different from the lives of the Blackfeet and Cheyennes who lived on the Great Plains, a vast region extending from central Texas in the south, to southern Canada in the north, and from the Mississippi River valley in the east, to the Rocky Mountains in the west.[3] Stories from nine different culture areas are included in this book to show these cultural differences.

Mythological tales about how animals helped to shape the universe, particularly trickster tales, often reveal how people lived and what was important in their lives. In "How Raven Steals Daylight from the Sky," for example, we learn that the Tsimshian people lived in dark cedar-plank houses, depended on salmon for food, and credited the trickster Raven for bringing daylight. In "The Moon Epic," we learn that the Coast Salish people also depended on salmon for food, but they credited the heavenly body Young Moon for putting salmon in the rivers to keep their people well fed.

Other tales are simple stories, and the plot *is* the story. "Tolowim-Woman" might be a cautionary tale, or a metaphor for death. It is the story of a woman who falls in love with and follows a beautiful butterfly. In the end, the chase kills her.

Native-American origin myths are unique in that they tell about how the world was created in a single tale. In the Cherokees' myth, "How the World Was Made," Beetle pulls mud up from under the water to create a suitable habitat for the Cherokee people, and Grandfather Buzzard flaps his wings to form the landscape.

I also include stories that explain the origin of special ceremonies. Among the Blackfeet people of the northern plains, the story about "Buffalo Husband" explains the origin of the annual buffalo dance. Hopi people of the desert southwest have a story, "The Kachinas Are Coming," about several of their kachinas, or spirit-beings, who grant wishes to young boys when they are hunting. These, and other kachinas, act as mediators between the living and the dead. They appear each year during the winter solstice celebrations wearing costumes and masks, and they dance to bring rain and prosperity.

Some American Indian tales tell about natural occurrences, or about the changing seasons. The Cheyennes' story, "Winter-Man's Fury," describes how Bow-in-Hand used his magic eagle-feather fan to drive heavy snow from the southern plains.

Another story, "Mandamin," is a fertility tale that tells about the care and nurturing of corn, which symbolizes the continuity of life.

In the story "Glooscap the Teacher," Glooscap is shown to be a hero who teaches the Micmac people all they need to know in order to succeed on earth, as well as how to reach the world beyond. His trickster side is also revealed in this myth.

American Indian oral traditions have kept these tales and many others like them alive for generations. I am grateful to the many devoted scholars, both Native-American and nonIndian, who have recorded the stories for all of us to share.

1

RAVEN STEALS DAYLIGHT FROM THE SKY

NORTHWEST (TSIMSHIANS)

INTRODUCTION

Two hundred years ago, European explorers sailed along the Pacific Northwest Coast from northern California to southern Alaska, and were awed by the huge cedar-plank houses and great dugout canoes that lined the shore. Women and children sat on narrow front porches weaving mats and clothing out of cedar bark. Men carved their family crests, similar to coats-of-arms, on great totem poles that flanked the front doors of their houses. The carvings on many totem poles included raven figures.

Tribes of the region traveled by boat from village to village because travel over the mountains was almost impossible. The Tsimshians lived in northwestern British Columbia along the Nass and Skeena rivers.[1] The Tsimshian people were famous for their expertly woven Chilkat blankets made out of goat's hair and cedar bark. They traded their blankets with bands of the Tlingits, who lived north of them.[2]

In summer, tribal life revolved around fishing activities. Men netted fish at sea and traveled upriver to spear salmon and halibut. Women filled drying racks in smokehouses with fish and tended the fires, which preserved the fish for winter storage.

In winter, the people settled into their great cedar-plank houses and prepared for communal feasts. Small feasts were held to celebrate the arrival of a new baby, or the occasion of a child's first naming ceremony. Larger ones, like the annual "potlatch," might honor an important person, celebrate a marriage, or mark the occasion of a house-raising. Whatever the reason, a festive mood filled the air, and whole villages came together to celebrate.

Today, many of these feasts are still celebrated by American Indians who live in the northwest.[3]

Storytelling remains an important part of traditional celebrations. Although some myths and legends belong to particular families, others, like the Raven story, belong to everyone. Inside the dark windowless plank houses of long ago, this story about how Raven brought daylight must have cheered up the occupants.[4]

RAVEN STEALS DAYLIGHT FROM THE SKY

Long, long ago the world was as black as Raven. It was so dark the Animal People often lost track of their children, bumped into one another looking for food, and had to talk constantly to stay together. This perpetual darkness made them very unhappy.

The Frog People sat in dugout wooden canoes and waited patiently for clear nights when bright stars would light up the waters. Then they went spearfishing. But they had to contend with Raven who harassed them constantly for food. Raven would swoop down toward the water when he heard a splash, hoping to snatch a fish off a spear. But the Frog Fishermen cleverly slapped the water at the opposite side of the boat to fool him.

Eventually, Raven grew tired of trying to be clever. He decided to go back to the sky where he came from and steal the box which held daylight. Then he and all the Animal People would be able to see where to find food.

So Raven flew up through a hole in the sky and walked until he came to the Sky Chief's house. There he waited beside the spring until the chief's only daughter came to fetch water. When Raven saw her coming down the path he quickly changed himself into a tiny cedar leaf and floated quietly on top of the water. The young girl was so thirsty she did not wait to set her cedar-bark bucket down on the ground. Instead, she held it out behind her, scooped up some water with her hand, and drank it. She did not notice the tiny cedar leaf that slipped down her throat along with the water.

Before long, the young girl had exciting news for her parents. "Mother. Father," she said. "I am with child."

For a long time, Sky Chief and his wife had feared that their only daughter would never give them a grandchild, so they were excited to hear this news. They waited patiently, and soon their daughter gave birth to a robust little boy. He had fine feathery black hair, keen dark eyes, and thin aquiline features.

Although the family loved the handsome baby, they could not seem to please him, no matter what they tried. The little boy refused to be held and struggled to get out of his mother's arms. His plump little body swaggered back and forth across the floor, and his loud cries filled the lodge.

Neither his mother nor his grandparents could figure out why their little boy was so unhappy. They washed him several times a day. They dressed and undressed him and brought him ample quantities of food. Still he squawked.

"We must seek the advice of our elders," said the chief. "Or else our grandson will grow into an unhappy adult."

Sky Chief walked through the village and invited the tribal elders to come to a meeting at his home. "Our grandson is very unhappy, and we do not know why. We seek your advice," he said.

The elders followed Sky Chief home. But some of them covered their ears in distress as they took seats around the room. Sky Chief's grandson crawled among the men, squawking louder than ever.

One elder picked up the boy and stroked his shiny

black hair. "What is it, child?" he asked. "What makes you so unhappy?" The baby screeched into the elder's face until the old man gently set him back down on the floor. Across the room another elder beckoned to the baby. "Come," he said. "Tell me why you cry." The chief's grandson went to where the old man sat, and then he crowed even louder. The old man fished frantically in his little bag for a handful of puffy cloud material with which he plugged his ears.

At last one of the elders, who had been watching the child very carefully, stood up. "It is the box you hang in the

corner that the boy wants," he declared to the chief and his daughter.

The box hanging in the corner was called the *mä*, and it held daylight. It had long been the chief's duty to protect its contents. "The box in the corner?" repeated Sky Chief. "That is the *mä*. He cannot have it."

But the little boy waddled over to where the box was hung, lifted his head, and began a long mournful cry.

"If you do not give him the box," said the elder. "He will cry until you do."

Sky Chief turned to his daughter. "I am afraid," he said.

"No one has ever played with the *mä* before? What if the box opens?"

"We must watch him very closely," said the boy's exhausted mother. Reluctantly, the chief took down the box and set it on the floor near the fire. At once the little boy stopped crying and wrapped his long curved arms around the box. A deafening silence filled the crowded lodge.

Sky Chief and his daughter smiled for the first time since the child had been born. With relief, the elders, also happy that the child had stopped squawking, pulled the stuffing out of their ears.

The boy tipped over the *mä*. Once. Twice. Three times. Then he tipped it back the other way. Once. Twice. Three times. He cooed like a contented little mourning dove.

The boy's delight with the precious box soon convinced Sky Chief and his daughter that the *mä* was safe with the strange little child. So they relaxed their watchfulness and went back to work. The little boy continued to coo as he tumbled the box around the lodge. Each day he worked himself closer and closer to the door. Then one day, without warning, the dark-haired little boy darted out of the lodge with the box on his shoulders.

When the Sky People saw him running away with the box they began to shout. "He is stealing the *mä*! Catch him! Catch him! He must not get away."

But Sky Chief's grandson disappeared as if he had wings. And once beyond reach of the Sky People, he vanished through the hole in the sky where he had entered many moons earlier. Before reaching earth, he changed back into Raven, took the *mä* off his shoulder, and clutched it in his strong talons. When Raven spotted the mouth of the Nass River, he flew upriver until he heard the voices of the Frog People.

"Please," he said to the Frog People, who were sitting

patiently in their dugout canoes, waiting for the stars to shine so they could see to spear fish. "Throw me a fish. I am very hungry."

But the fishermen knew that Raven was always hungry and always wanted others to feed him. "Catch your own fish, you lazy thing," replied one of the fishermen.

Raven asked again.

The fishermen continued to ignore him.

Raven just wanted something to eat before he opened the box of daylight. "You will be sorry if you do not feed me," he threatened. "I have brought you something very special. But I am very hungry, and I must eat first."

"You cannot fool us," said one of the fishermen. "You are Raven the trickster and nothing but a liar. And all you want is free food."

Raven protested, "I have brought you daylight in this box. And I made a long, dangerous journey to bring it to earth so that our people will never be hungry again. But I will not give it to you until you give me something to eat."

The Frog People laughed.

Raven waited until they began fishing under the light of the stars before he issued his last warning to the Frog People: "I will wait no longer. If you throw me a fish you will not be punished. But if you do not, you will be very sorry."

This time the fishermen did not even bother to look up. They were too busy spearing fish.

Then Raven gripped the box in his strong talons, lifted it off the ground, and glided gracefully along the water's edge. If the Frog People had looked up, they might have seen his shiny purple-green wings glistening in the starlight. But they did not. Not until he dropped the box onto the rocky shore.

When Raven did this, daylight came flying out of the broken box in all directions. It flashed out over the mountains. It whirled up through the valleys. And it sliced through the freshwater rivers and streams of the region. Animal People all over the land were surprised and delighted. But not the Frog People, who had not believed Raven's box held daylight. Now they were frightened.

Shortly after all the light had left the box, North Wind began to blow violently against the little boats that held the Frog People. It blew so hard they were swept out to sea, and their little canoes slammed into the side of a steep rocky island. When the Frog People tried to climb up the cliffs, North Wind froze them in place, so that they would never again be concerned about daylight.

The other Animal People cheered for Raven and called him a hero. And no one ever went hungry again, especially not Raven.

QUESTIONS AND ANSWERS

Q: Why did Raven steal the box of daylight?

A: There was no light on earth, and the Animal People had a difficult time finding food. Raven, who had always tricked others into feeding him, decided to go back to the sky where he came from and steal daylight. That way, the Animal People could find food more easily, and he would have less trouble begging for it.

Q: What happened when the box of daylight dropped and broke open?

A: When the box of daylight slammed down on the rocky shore, it lit up the land so brightly that the Animal People could see to find food.

Q: Why do the Tsimshian people carve Raven figures on the totem poles that guard their doorways?

A: Raven brought daylight to the people and made himself a hero. His blackness is a reminder of perpetual night. Fish were the staple food of the Tsimshian people, and Raven's image reminds them of how impossible it would be to fish if the world were as dark as his large black body.

Q: Describe the two different settings in the story. Why was Raven able to visit both places?

A: One setting is the homeland of the Tsimshian people. The other is the sky where Raven went to steal daylight. Raven was a godlike figure who had the ability to travel between both worlds. He could be both good and bad, but the Frog People knew him only as an earthly trickster.

EXPERT COMMENTARY

Franz Boas lived among the tribes of the Pacific Northwest from 1886 to 1931. During his stay with the people he recorded many of their myths and legends, especially different versions of the Raven story. In his book *Race, Language and Culture*, Boas comments on the Tsimshian version of how Raven steals the daylight:

> It will be seen that the main characteristic of these [Raven] tales is the fact that the Raven gave the world its present shape while trying to satisfy his own wants, and that he employed fair means and foul to reach his own selfish ends. While his actions benefit mankind, he is not prompted by altruistic [unselfish] motives, but only by the desire to satisfy his own needs. I find in most tales of the transformer [a mythological character who can do either good or evil], or of the culture hero, the prime motive is, as in this particular case, a purely egotistical [self-centered] one, and that the changes which actually benefit mankind are only incidentally beneficial. They are primarily designed by the transformer to reach his own selfish ends.[5]

In his book *Historical Atlas of World Mythology*, Joseph Campbell, an eminent scholar of world mythology, wrote of the Raven tales:

> Only in the interior [North American] was the role of Raven taken over by other trickster figures: in the Woodlands by the Great Hare, and on the Plains by Coyote. In the Arctic, his adventures are recalled in folktales half-remembered, while on the Pacific Coast, the full mythology survives, reflected in works of an extraordinary art and enacted in great, masked, mid-winter ceremonials. . . . Throughout. . . the Raven Cycle of the Tsimshian, there is an atmosphere of . . . magic and wonder that is far stronger than anything surviving. . . .[6]

2

THE MOON EPIC
COAST PLATEAU (SALISH)

INTRODUCTION

More than three hundred years ago, explorers Lewis and Clark discovered that the fertile coastal plain that extends along the Pacific Coast from Alaska to Mexico was walled off from the interior of the country by tall rugged mountains. There were only two possible passages through the mountains: one in the south where the Sierra Nevada Mountains meet the Mojave Desert; the other in the north where the Columbia River cuts a path to the sea. Lewis and Clark decided to take the northern passage, and there they met the Salish people:

> . . . the grandest and most pleasing prospects which my eyes ever surveyed, in my frount [sic] a boundless Ocean; to the N. and N.E. the coast as. . . far as my sight could be extended, the Seas rageing with emence wave[s] and brakeing with great force from the rocks of Cape Disapointment as far as I could see to the N.W.[1]

Coast Salish tribes, who once occupied much of the region around Puget Sound off the coast of Washington State, enjoyed a unique blend of rushing white water, moist mountain meadows, and flat open valleys. Men speared migrating salmon, which they called "dog salmon," from cliffs above the Columbia River. Dog salmon is another name for Pacific Coast salmon (gorbuscha), chuna, or keta salmon. Women dug up camass bulbs, the edible root of a slender hyacinth-type wildflower that grows in high mountain meadows.

The dog salmon were smoked, and the camass bulbs were dried and stored away for winter. During these cold, damp days and nights a favorite tale was told about Young Moon, a mythological hero who lived in both the sky and on earth, who created the animals, including humans; ordered day and night; and filled the rivers with salmon.[2]

THE MOON EPIC

<×◆×◆×◆×◆×◆×◆×◆◆×◆×◆×◆×◆×◆×◆×◆◆×◆×◆×◆×◆×◆×◆>

Old Moon had two daughters who were devoted to each other. They shared chores at home, dug wild camass bulbs in the mountain meadows together, and whispered their secrets back and forth.

One day, after they had spent more time talking than digging, it became too dark to go home. So they settled down among the tall blue and white camass flowers to spend the night. But the sisters could not sleep. Instead, they lay awake staring up at the thick black sky that sparkled with tiny stars.

"Oh how I would like to marry that shiny white star over there," said the younger girl.

Her older sister smiled and said, "I would like to marry that bright little red one over there."

The next morning when the sisters awoke they were no longer in the field of camass flowers but seated in the sky next to their chosen star husbands. The older sister smiled at the strong young man with long black hair and bright red eyes who sat beside her. But the younger sister gasped when she looked beside her and saw the gnarled old man with long white hair and a tangled beard.

All around them were Star People—men, women, and

children of all sizes and shapes. Some of them were handsome, others not so attractive, but all of them were kind. The women took the sisters to a meadow in the sky that was blanketed with beautiful camass flowers just like the one they had left on earth. They gave the sisters digging sticks and told them to dig up small bulbs, but not ones that grew too deeply.

The sisters did as they were told and went out each day and filled their baskets with bulbs. But they missed their family and friends on earth. Their husbands tried to make them forget their sadness, but they could not. The younger sister was especially homesick, as she yearned for a man her own age.

One day, after the sisters began digging, the older one whispered, "I am with child, dear sister." The younger girl hugged her and wept. She was happy for her older sister, but sad that she would never have a child of her own. That evening the younger sister disguised her weeping by sitting in front of the fire so that smoke blew in her face.

Still the sisters dug camass bulbs every day. One morning the younger sister asked, "Why do you think we must not dig bulbs that grow deeply?"

"I do not know," said the other. "Shall we try and find out?" So they searched until they came upon a bulb that was long and grew deep down. "I have one," said the younger sister, and she dug gently all around the bulb, removing the dirt as she dug. When she finally pulled it out, a great blast of cold air rushed up through the hole it had left in the sky. The girls peered down through the hole and saw their family and friends below. "This is the reason we were told not to dig up bulbs that grow deep down," said the older sister. "Now we must make plans to escape. We will make a ladder, drop it down through the hole, and climb down to earth."

The next day when the girls went to the sky meadow, they dug camass bulbs part of the time and collected long tough vines the rest of the time. Day after day they collected more and more vines and twisted them into a long ladder. But each time they dropped it through the hole in the sky, it was too short.

Then one day, a baby boy, whom they named Young Moon, was born to the older sister. The girls, who wanted Young Moon to grow up among his own people on earth, now had even more reason to complete their ladder. They took turns caring for Young Moon, digging roots, and collecting vines.

Finally, one day when the younger sister dropped the

ladder it touched the earth. She cried out excitedly and jumped up and hugged her sister.

"You go first. I will hand you the baby and follow," said the older sister. After they were all safely on the ladder the older girl pulled some cedar boughs over the hole so that a forest would grow over the meadow and their husbands would not know where to look for them.

When the news spread on earth that the children of Old Moon and his wife had returned home, the villagers gathered to celebrate. "Go with your family and friends," said the old blind grandmother. "I will take care of your son." The older sister propped the cradleboard with her sleeping son against a large tree and thanked the old lady.

No one knew that Dog Salmon, an ugly salmon with large teeth and a protruding jaw, was thrashing about beneath the bushes waiting to steal the child. After the old woman dozed off, Dog Salmon took Young Moon out of his cradleboard, tucked him under his murky brown jacket, and put a rotten log in the child's place.

After the celebration was over, Young Moon's mother came back to get him. "Oh," she screamed. "My son. My son. Where are you? Look at this rotten log in my son's cradleboard," she said throwing the log on the ground. "Please everyone—Woodpecker, Bluejay, Raven—you must help me find Young Moon."

Bluejay arrived first. He was the only one who knew that Young Moon held great powers, and the only one who knew where to look for the kidnapped baby. He flicked his round-tipped black and white tail in the air, and called, "Sassy. Sassy. Sassy."

Within minutes Woodpecker alighted on a bush beside the worried mother. He bobbed his head up and down as if trying to toss off the black mustache that circled his little beak. He was eager to join Bluejay.

Raven, the most clever of the birds, heard the young mother's plea and figured there might be some meat for him if he joined the chase. He flapped his huge black wings, stuck his wedge-shaped tail in the air, and headed off to join the others.

After the birds had left to find Young Moon, his mother went down to the river to wash out his cedar-bark diaper. After she had rinsed it several times she heard a noise. There standing before her was a handsome little dark-haired boy. "I have come to console you. I am Sun, brother of Young Moon," he said. "Be patient and do not worry. Bluejay will find him."

Meanwhile, Bluejay had flown to where sky and earth

come together. Back and forth, back and forth he flew, looking for a hole to fly through. At last he found one and tried to squeeze his head underneath, but the hole was too small, and he crushed his crest of fine blue feathers. Cocky Raven was sure he could get through by sheer force, so he stuck his fat beak in the hole and pushed and pushed. But nothing happened. Woodpecker tried to peck a hole in the sky, but that did not work. Then he tried to peck one in the earth. That did not work, either. The sky and earth were firmly locked together. Discouraged, Woodpecker and Raven flew home.

But Bluejay would not give up. He stayed and waited for many years until he found an opening large enough to squirm through. Then he traveled far and wide until he found Young Moon who was living in the sky with the Dog Salmon People. "So this is where the Dog Salmon live," said Bluejay. "And it is they who kidnapped you so long ago. We have been very worried about you. You must come home to earth and use your power to transform things for our people."

Young Moon hung his head. The Dog Salmon People had always lived in the sky, and he did not know if he could convince them to follow him to earth. "I will need time to think," said Young Moon to Bluejay. "I will come when the time is right."

Young Moon thought for many days. At last he called the Dog Salmon People together and asked them to come home with him. He promised to put them in the great clear-water rivers that flowed out of the mountains and into the Pacific Ocean along the Northwest Coast if they would agree to be food for his people.

The Dog Salmon People agreed. At first they swam downriver, but Young Moon turned them around and showed them how to swim upstream against the current.

Then he traveled easily over the land, and he changed many things along the way on his journey home.

The first strange-looking creatures he encountered were fighting. He turned them into birds and stones. The next group, little birds who ran around stupidly, he made into sandpipers. A group of fishermen in a canoe on a lake he turned into sawbill ducks, and others, standing in shallow water, he made into mallard ducks. The last group of creatures, whom he could not identify, were lounging on the beach, so he turned them into clams.

After Young Moon had changed everything he encountered on earth, he created a great waterfall to challenge the Dog Salmon on their way upstream. When he finally arrived at home, his family waited to cheer him. Young Moon was pleased with himself.

"I will show you my great powers," he boasted to his family and friends. "Which one of you would like to be Sun by day and Moon by night?" Raven tried out for Moon. But he failed. Woodpecker tried out for Sun. And he failed.

"I am afraid that my brother and I will have to do these jobs ourselves," said Young Moon. So he called his brother Sun and asked him to give the people bright warm light during the day. Sun was a great success, and the people were very happy. Moon rose after Sun was gone and made a long slow journey across the night sky. Again, the people were pleased.

"Before I take my place in the sky forever," said Young Moon, "I must finish my work on earth." Then he created the humans and placed them along the rivers and streams of the region, where they have fished for Dog Salmon ever since.

QUESTIONS AND ANSWERS

Q: Which sister married a good-looking young star-man?

A: The older sister.

Q: Why was the younger sister disappointed with her new husband?

A: He was old and ugly and would not be able to give her children.

Q: Why did the Sky People tell the sisters not to dig up bulbs that grew too deep?

A: They knew if the girls dug too deep they would open up a hole in the sky and see earth below them.

Q: How did the sisters escape back to earth?

A: They gathered vines and wove them into a long ladder.

Q: How would you describe the younger sister?

A: She was an understanding and accepting young woman. Even though she was unhappy with an old man for a husband and disappointed that she would never have children of her own, she took care of her little nephew like he was a son.

Q: Why was a Dog Salmon character chosen to kidnap Young Moon?

A: Dog Salmon would later return to earth and be the most important food for Young Moon's people.

Q: Describe Raven's behavior.

A: He is self-centered and lazy. He joins the chase in hopes of finding fresh meat for himself, but returns home when it requires too much effort.

Q: Describe Woodpecker.

A: He has the characteristics of both Bluejay and Raven. Woodpecker is eager to help find Young Moon, but not willing to try as hard as Bluejay.

Q: Describe Bluejay's character.

A: He is responsible and persistent. He does not give up trying to get through a hole between the earth and the sky because he knows that Young Moon possesses special powers.

Q: Why did Young Moon take the Dog Salmon People to earth with him?

A: Young Moon did not want to leave the Dog Salmon People behind in the sky, so he offered to take them to earth with him. He promised to let them swim freely in the rivers of the region if they would be food for his people. The Dog Salmon People agreed.

Q: Why is Young Moon a godlike figure in the story?

A: He acts like a creator when he creates the animals, including man; orders night and day; and makes Dog Salmon a source of food for his people.

EXPERT COMMENTARY

Franz Boas, an author who was also a professor of anthropology at Columbia University for many years, wrote in *Race, Language and Culture*:

> On the north Pacific Coast the notions regarding the universe are on the whole vague and contradictory; nevertheless visits to the sky play an important role in the tales. The ideas regarding a ladder leading to heaven, and journeys across the ocean to fabulous countries, also enter into the make-up of the Northwest Coast traditions.[3]

John Bierhorst has been writing and translating American Indian myths, tales, and poetry for many years. In his book *The Mythology of North America*, he recounts an Indian's comments about the Moon Epic that were recorded in the 1920s:

> I am an Indian today. Moon has given us fish and game. The white people have come and overwhelmed us. We may not kill a deer nor catch a fish forbidden by white men to be taken. I should like any of these lawmakers to tell me if Moon or Sun has set him here to forbid our people to kill game given to us by Moon and Sun. Though white people overwhelm us, it is Moon that placed us here, and the laws we are bound to obey are those established by Moon in the ancient time.[4]

3

TOLOWIM-WOMAN AND BUTTERFLY-MAN

CALIFORNIA (MAIDU)

INTRODUCTION

The natural resources of California were once so great that they supported a large population of American Indians who did not need to farm. There were fish, shellfish, and sea mammals along the coast, and deer, tule elk, and pronghorn antelope in the valleys. Fertile oak trees grew everywhere, and acorns, their fruit, were the staple food of the region. Women ground the acorns in stone mortars, washed the tannic acid out of the flour, and added the clean meal to their stews. They also made acorn pancakes from the flour.

In northeastern California, the Maidu people lived in large winter houses dug partly underground and covered with grass mats and earth. Small settlements were linked together by the same well-worn trails that led to the ceremonial lodge located in the largest and most centrally located community.

Men spent much of their time hunting and fishing, and women gathered large quantities of acorns, which they stored away for winter.

Each autumn, in September or October, the Maidu people practiced mourning ceremonies in honor of the dead. Families wailed, cried, and sang for several nights while rites were performed for dead relatives. One night was reserved for the burning of personal possessions. This ceremony was designed to give the possessions over to those who had recently died. Families who missed their dead relatives encouraged their ghosts to linger around after the ceremony was over, although the living had to promise not to look directly at the dead, since the sight of a ghost could be fatal to a living person.[1]

When the Maidu say "one's heart is gone away," they mean that person is dead.[2] Tolowim-Woman's story is the only one of its kind. It is believed the storyteller made her belong to a fictitious tribe, named Tolowim, because a story about a woman who would abandon her husband and child is too shameful to belong to the Maidu people.[3]

TOLOWIM-WOMAN
AND BUTTERFLY-MAN

Long ago, a young girl they called Tolowim-Woman lived in a large pit-house that was nestled in the California foothills. She was a dutiful wife and mother and did her share of the sewing and acorn-grinding. But the long hours of darkness indoors, when the only light came from the flame of the fire, made her restless and moody. She wanted to be outdoors running free.

In spring, Tolowim-Woman's young husband went off to greet the salmon as they began their journey inland from the sea. She stayed at home to care for their young son and to do chores with the other women. But she longed to go into the hills and walk among the fresh bright-colored spring irises.

One day, while the women of the lodge were busy chatting among themselves, Tolowim-Woman put on her new buckskin dress, picked up her young son, whom she called Aki, and slipped quietly out the door. She set his cradleboard on the ground and knelt down to position it behind her. She secured the tumpline, the wide strap that fit around her forehead to help support the cradleboard, and raised her son onto her back. Then she stepped lightly along the narrow path that led up into the hills.

Springtime was Tolowim-Woman's favorite time of year. She remembered her own mother carrying her up the same path in her cradleboard, and she remembered the little grey squirrels that darted back and forth behind her mother's back showing off their quickness.

Tolowim-Woman swung her arms high in the air as if the sky were her roof and her home had no boundaries. Her fine black hair brushed against her shoulders, and her small bare feet pressed gently into grass that was still wet from the morning dew. She was free and happy. She skipped along the well-worn path as if she carried no burden. If her son was heavy it did not matter because her heart was light.

"Look, Aki," she said. "The sparrow hawk is soaring the air currents. Isn't he beautiful?" Even though her young son was only nine moons old and could not speak, Tolowim-Woman knew he understood.

She continued to throw words back over her shoulder as she walked. Then, as the sun climbed high in the clear afternoon sky, Tolowim-Woman's pace slackened. She was getting tired, so she set the cradleboard down against a giant oak tree and sat down beside it.

"Isn't it beautiful up here in the hills?" she asked. Aki's open smiling face was her answer. Tolowim-Woman laughed and realized it would be just as beautiful when the leaves began to fall and they would return to this spot to gather acorns.

Then Tolowim-Woman stood up and began to twirl around like a leaf in the breeze. Aki's large brown eyes followed his mother as she whirled gaily around and around in circles.

While Tolowim-Woman twirled, a large black butterfly fluttered playfully around her. It brushed her extended arms. First one. Then the other. Then it floated over to where Aki's cradleboard leaned against the tree and fluttered in front of the little boy's happy face.

Tolowim-Woman stopped dancing when she heard her young son squealing. The handsome black butterfly circled around the oak tree showing off the tiny white circles that glowed above several reddish crossbars outlined on its wings. (These are the markings of a red admiral butterfly.) "You are so lovely," she whispered. Then, impulsively, she reached out to grab it. But the handsome black butterfly quickly flew away.

Tolowim-Woman believed she had not been quick enough. She took a couple of steps toward it and tried again. And again. And again. Still the butterfly fluttered from one bush to another, staying just beyond her reach.

The handsome young butterfly drifted higher and higher into the hills. Tolowim-Woman wanted this butterfly more than she had ever wanted anything before. She could not stop chasing it. "Please," she pleaded. "If you will wait for me I will go away with you."

For a moment the great black wings seemed not to move. Then the handsome butterfly drifted downward and came to rest on a young manzanita bush. It did not move when Tolowim-Woman approached. But when she was close enough to reach out, it flew away. Tolowim-Woman climbed over rocks, walked through brambles, and tripped on rotted tree stumps. Her legs became bloody, her long black hair tangled with grass and twigs, and the fringes on her new buckskin dress became torn. Still she could not stop chasing the butterfly.

At last, the sun slipped down behind the hills and her pace slowed. Exhausted, she sank down onto the ground. She called to the handsome butterfly, "I am too tired to follow you any longer."

Slowly the black wings began to flutter, and the

handsome young butterfly made a great wide circle in the air. It turned back and flew to the spot where Tolowim-Woman sat.

This time she did not reach out but watched quietly as it came closer and closer. When it landed on the ground beside her, it was no longer a butterfly but a handsome young man wearing only a thin band of white cloth around his head and a small apron held on by a narrow band of red around his waist.

Tolowim-Woman gasped, "You are the most handsome man I have ever seen."

Butterfly-Man smiled, sat down beside her, and took her in his arms. They laid down together on the fresh warm grass and remained there until morning.

When Butterfly-Man awoke, he asked Tolowim-Woman, "Will you come home with me?"

"Oh yes," she replied. "I will follow you wherever you go." Love made her forget the husband she had left at home and the child whose cradleboard still leaned against an oak tree far away. All she could think about was the beautiful young man by her side, and the freedom they would share together.

"Come," said Butterfly-Man, "I will take you to the land of my people. But it is a most dangerous journey. We must walk through the Valley of Butterflies, and they will all want to take you away from me. But you must not let them." He took her fingers and wrapped them around the band of red that circled his waist. "I will lead you through the valley safely, but you must not look at any of the butterflies. And you must never let go of me. If you do, I will lose my power to protect you."

Tolowim-Woman held on with both hands, and the couple set off toward the Valley of Butterflies. Before they were halfway down the valley, butterflies of every shape,

size, and color began to surround them. Tolowim-Woman kept her eyes focused downward as she walked, and she tightened her grip on Butterfly-Man's waist. Butterflies fluttered in front of her face. They circled her head, and brushed against her hair. Still she refused to look up.

Tolowim-Woman and Butterfly-Man traveled for many hours through great swarms of butterflies. Then, a bold black and orange one (a monarch butterfly), larger and stronger than Butterfly-Man, refused to go away. It flew back and forth in front of Tolowim-Woman's downcast eyes, and when she would not open them it lit boldly on her trembling lower lip.

Tolowim-Woman could not remain composed any longer and made tiny slits in her eyes to take a look. The butterfly's bright orange wings brushed lightly against her nose and tickled her. Instinctively, she reached for it. But before she could close her grip, it flew away.

Even though Tolowim-Woman feared that Butterfly-Man's power to protect her might be lost, she could not stop reaching toward the brilliant black and orange wings that fluttered before her. Butterfly-Man remained silent. Tolowim-Woman continued to reach out with her free hand. Butterfly-Man's pace increased.

Before long, hundreds of other butterflies, each one stronger and more beautiful than the next, began to swarm around them. Tolowim-Woman could not restrain herself. She reached for one. Then another. And another.

"You are all so beautiful," she said as they whirled around her. "I want all of you." Slowly the other hand slipped from Butterfly-Man's waist, and she began to grab at butterflies in all directions. But each time she thought she had captured one, it escaped from her grasp. Butterfly-Man continued walking. Faster. And faster. And faster. Tolowim-Woman continued to reach for butterflies in every direction.

"Wait," she cried. "I am coming. Wait for me."

Tolowim-Woman ran. And called out for Butterfly-Man. And kept reaching out for butterflies as she went. But Butterfly-Man did not slow down. Nor did he turn around. Before long, Tolowim-Woman's heart was gone away.

QUESTIONS AND ANSWERS

Q: Why does Tolowim-Woman wish to change her life?

A: Her life is monotonous and confining. Her husband is always away from home, and she must do the chores expected of a woman of the tribe. She longs to be outdoors and free of responsibility.

Q: What qualities does Butterfly-Man possess, and what do they represent to Tolowim-Woman?

A: Butterfly-Man's great beauty represents the attraction of sensual pleasures. He is Tolowim-Woman's guide to freedom. He flies freely in an enchanted and beautiful land without any responsibilities.

Q: What is the symbolism of Butterfly-Man's color? Why is he represented as a black butterfly?

A: Among many peoples of the world, the color black is the symbol of death. The handsome black butterfly may be such a symbol. One could say that Tolowim-Woman left her husband and child because she loved death more than life. It could be a metaphor for loss of this world.

Q: Name the consequences of Tolowim-Woman's butterfly chase.

A: She abandons her husband and son, then fails to obey Butterfly-Man. Ultimately, she loses her life, both literally and figuratively. Her quest for pure freedom results in the loss of her material existence.

Q: What is the moral of the story?

A: By wanting too much, one risks losing what one already has.

Q: If Tolowim-Woman had obeyed Butterfly-Man, could she have achieved the freedom she was seeking? Was it her failure to obey him that caused her death, or simply following him in the first place?

A: The storyteller does not reveal the answers to these questions. How would you answer them?

EXPERT COMMENTARY

In the early part of this century, A. L. Kroeber lived for seventeen years among the Indians of California and did fifteen years of research on his book *Handbook of the Indians of California*. He was one of the foremost figures of his generation in the field of American anthropology, and this book is considered one of his most important works. In it he writes:

> What we call the soul, the Maidu named heart. "His heart is gone away" means that a person is dead. In a swoon or in a dream a person's heart leaves his body.
>
> . . . The northern valley people believe that a dead person's heart lingers near the body for several days. It then journeys to every spot which the living person had visited, retracing each of his steps and reenacting every deed performed in life. This accomplished, the spirit seeks a mysterious cavern in the Marysville Buttes, the great spirit mountain of the Maidu, where for the first time it eats spirit food and is washed. Its experiences here are a repetition of those of the first man of mythology. From the Marysville Buttes the spirit ascends to the sky land, flower land, or spirit land, as it is variously called.[4]

In her book *Inland Whale*, Theodora Kroeber, wife of A.L. Kroeber, says of the human aspects of the story:

> . . . And the fantasy of the butterfly as man in disguise would seem to me a woman's fantasy.
>
> . . . That the Tolowim-Woman's story lives on amidst literary company strange to it may be because it continues to remind Maidu women of lonely excursions into the hills, of private daydreams of their own, of a butterfly-filled land.[5]

4

HOW THE WORLD WAS MADE

SOUTHEAST (CHEROKEES)

INTRODUCTION

The Cherokee people occupied a vast territory in the rugged southern Appalachian Mountains. In the nearby foothills, deer, elk, bears, turkeys, and other animals fed in the dense hemlock, pine, and spruce forests. Freshwater rivers and streams plentifully stocked with fish flowed across rich valleys. The Cherokees successfully combined farming with hunting and the gathering of wild food. While men hunted game, women collected quantities of wild grapes, blackberries, huckleberries, wild roots, and nuts in season. With assistance from the men, women raised corn, beans, squash, pumpkins, sunflowers, and other cultivated crops.

The Cherokees lived in large towns that were organized in sophisticated political units. Their houses were made of small trees woven between upright posts and plastered with clay. This building style is called wattle and daub. A central council house and open plaza were reserved for religious ceremonies and festivities.

The Cherokees believed that the sun, moon, and stars were spiritual beings and that the animals, too, had spirits. Some southeastern tribes regarded the sun as a male spirit, but the Cherokees generally depicted the sun as female.[1] In the Cherokee creation story, "How the World Was Made," Grandfather Buzzard shapes wet earth, brought up from the bottom of an endless sea, with his wings, making mountains and valleys. Birds represent the Upper World, which the Cherokees associate with the past. Fish represent fertility, which the Cherokees associate with the future.[2]

How the World
Was Made

<◆×◆×◆×◆×◆×◆><◆×◆×◆×◆×◆×◆><◆×◆×◆×◆×◆×◆>

When all the world was water, the animals lived in the sky
beyond the rainbow where everyone complained about
being cramped for space. "It is much too crowded up
here," said Grandfather Buzzard. "Why don't we find out
what is down there under the water?"

"I will go. I will go," clicked Beetle as he extended his
little forelegs as far as they would go.

Grandfather Buzzard agreed that since Beetle
belonged in the water, he should go. "See what you can
find down there," said Grandfather Buzzard, and he waved
good-bye.

Beetle dove from the sky and floated slowly to earth.
He landed on top of the water and whirled around and
around and around. When he found an opening in the
surface, he kicked his little hind legs in the air and dove
under. After awhile, Beetle surfaced, his forelegs coated
with soft mud.

Beetle's friends watched from above as the mud from
under the water spread out in all directions. The mass of
mud grew, and grew, and kept on growing, until it was a
great big island. Then it was magically tied to the sky with
four sturdy ropes.

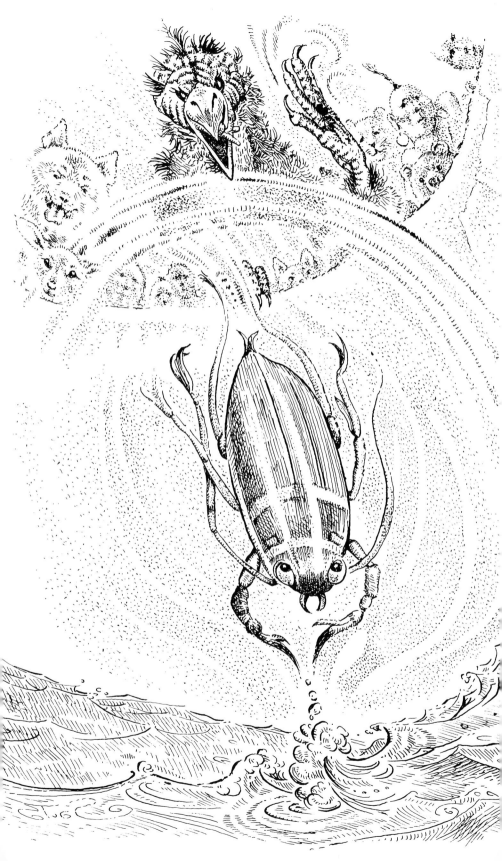

Beetle returned home pleased with his good work. "When the mud dries," he said, "there will be much land for us to share. We will never be crowded again."

The others in the sky saw that the mud was still soft and wet. Everyone waited for the land to dry out. At last Raven grew impatient. "Why don't we just go down and try it out?" he asked. Bluejay flicked his blue and white tail and hopped forward. "I want to go," he said, "but perhaps I am too small to undertake such a long journey."

"Do not worry," said Grandfather Buzzard, "you are quick and clever. You will make it."

Bluejay flew to earth. He traveled north, south, east, and west. Everywhere the island's mud was wet and sticky. "It is too soon," reported Bluejay when he returned to the sky. "Our feet will get stuck if we try to land down there now."

Old Man Owl closed his big round eyes and went back to sleep. Mountain Lion curled up in a clump of grass and sighed. The trees let their leaves fall to the ground in disgust. Everyone was disappointed.

The animals busied themselves in the sky while they waited for their little mud island to dry out. Then one day Grandfather Buzzard stood up firm and tall. His big black body swayed, and his feathers rippled. "I have waited long enough," he declared in a loud voice. "I am going down to take a look for myself."

No one ever challenged Grandfather Buzzard. Instead, they watched as he flapped his huge wings and flew down to earth. The long journey made the old bird very tired, and he sank lower and lower and closer to the ground. When he was as low as he could get without actually landing, the flapping of his wings carved out great long valleys wherever they touched the soft earth. And where his wings swept upward, they created tall rugged mountains.

The animals watched from above. "We have got to get Grandfather Buzzard back up here," said Bluejay. "Look what he is doing. He is creating too many mountains."

Grandfather Buzzard finally returned to the sky. He strutted among the animals with his chest puffed out. "The mud is not completely dry," he admitted. "But one has to admit that it is very much more interesting down there since I have visited."

Bluejay rolled his eyes. "That remains to be seen," he muttered. For a long time afterward, the animals took turns checking to see if the earth had hardened. But each time they returned home they were sorry to report that the land was still too soft.

A long time passed before Grandfather Buzzard spoke again. "I think it is time to descend," he said. "Look how solid those mountains are. And see how the water has formed into long ribbons that flow through the valleys. The land is ready. We must go."

Bluejay, Hawk, Crow, Magpie, and a stream of little songbirds fluffed up their wings in readiness for the flight. Mountain Lion, Panther, Deer, Fox, and all the other animals preened themselves in preparation for the trip. The trees pulled themselves up by their roots and wrapped themselves up in tight little bundles so that they, too, would be prepared to move.

At last Grandfather Buzzard led off, and the others followed. Indeed, he was right. The earth was not too hard and not too soft. It was just right. There was only one problem: It was totally dark.

"Oh my," said Grandfather Buzzard. "I did not count on this. I must grab Sun from up there beyond the rainbow."

So Grandfather Buzzard went back and got hold of Sun. "I will show you how to behave," he said to Sun in his firmest voice. "Start here in the east and travel toward the west every day across the island."

Sun did as she was told and lit up the land exactly as Grandfather Buzzard had told her to do. But the animals were not at all happy. Sun was too close and too hot.

"Sun must be moved away," complained Crawfish. "Look what has happened to the shell on my back. It is scorched, and now I am bright red. My flesh is spoiled." So Grandfather Buzzard pushed Sun higher up into the sky. Still things did not cool off. So he pushed Sun higher and higher above the land.

"There," said Grandfather Buzzard. "That looks like a good distance." But the animals still complained. After many attempts, he finally got Sun in just the right position under the arch of the rainbow. "Now," said Grandfather Buzzard to Sun, "travel from east to west across the island each day." Again Sun did as she was told, and this time everyone was happy.

The animals and plants were barely settled when Grandfather Buzzard announced that they must stay awake for seven nights. (Seven is a sacred number to the Cherokees because it represents the directional units of the world: east, west, north, and south, as well as up, down, and here.) So the animals and plants tried their best. The first night was easy, and everyone stayed awake. But on the second night several of the animals fell asleep. On the third night even more of them fell asleep. And by the seventh night Owl, Panther, and only a few others were able to remain awake.

As a result, Owl and Panther were given the ability to see at night and prey on others who could not. Cedar, Pine, Spruce, Holly, and Laurel trees, who also stayed awake the whole seven nights, got to keep their leaves all year round, and to hold strong medicines. The trees that fell asleep too soon were made to lose their leaves before winter came.

After the plants and animals were in place, a young brother and sister arrived. At first it was only the two of them. Then one day the brother hit his sister with a fish, (the Cherokees' symbol for fertility), and told her to multiply. Seven days later, the sister bore a child. And seven days later another child was born. Thereafter, every seven days she bore another child. The children arrived so often everyone was frightened the earth would become as crowded as the sky had been.

So, afterward, the woman was made to have only one child a year. And it has been that way ever since.

QUESTIONS AND ANSWERS

Q: What part did Beetle and Grandfather Buzzard play in shaping the landscape of the Cherokee people?

A: Beetle brought mud up from under the water to create fertile land masses, and Grandfather Buzzard flapped his wings to create mountains and valleys.

Q: Why does Crawfish complain about being scorched by the sun?

A: His vanity is upset by having been turned a bright red color.

Q: Why does Grandfather Buzzard tell the plants and animals they must remain awake for seven nights?

A: Seven is a sacred number for the Cherokee people. It symbolizes the units of the world—the seven directions: east, west, north, and south, as well as up, down, and here.

Q: Name the trees in the story that stayed awake and were allowed to keep their leaves all year? What kind of trees are they?

A: Cedar, Pine, Spruce, Holly, and Laurel stayed awake the prescribed time. These are called evergreen trees.

Q: What happened to the trees that could not manage to stay awake?

A: The trees that did not stay awake were made to lose their leaves each fall. They are called deciduous trees.

Q: What do fish symbolize to the Cherokee people?

A: Fish symbolize fertility and the future. By hitting his sister with a fish, the boy gave the girl the power to populate the land.

EXPERT COMMENTARY

James Mooney launched his career with the Bureau of American Ethnology in 1885. Until his death in 1921, Mooney traveled among Native Americans who lived in the southeast, recording important historical information told to him by the Indians themselves. He lived in the mountains of western North Carolina among the eastern band of Cherokees for parts of the years 1887–1890 and on and off thereafter. His work is much respected by both Native-American and nonIndian scholars.

> From decay of the old tradition and admixtures of Bible ideas the Cherokee genesis [creation] myth is too far broken down to be recovered excepting in disjointed fragments.
>
> . . . The incident of the buzzard shaping the mountains occurs also in the genesis myth of the Creeks and Yuchi, southern neighbors of the Cherokee, but by them the first earth is said to have been brought up from under the water by the crawfish.[3]

Charles Hudson, a distinguished professor of anthropology, has written numerous books about the southeastern Indians. He says about the Cherokees' various worlds:

> The Southeastern Indians conceived of This World as a great, flat island resting rather precariously on the surface of the waters, suspended from the vault of the sky by four cords attached at each of the cardinal directions.
>
> . . . Above This World was the sky vault, an inverted bowl of solid rock which rose and fell twice each day, at dawn and at dusk, so that the sun and moon could pass beneath it. When the sun passed up and under the inside of the sky vault it was day; while it was returning back to its starting place in the east it was night.[4]

In the beginning, just two worlds existed: the Upper World and the Under World. This World, the world on which the Indians live, was created later. The Upper World epitomized order and expectableness, while the Under World epitomized disorder and change, and This World stood somewhere between perfect order and complete chaos.[5]

In his book *The Mythology of North America*, John Bierhorst writes about the Cherokees:

Cooperation among animals—the council-of-animals theme—recurs in major creation myths of the Cherokee, Yuchi, and other tribes. According to a nineteenth-century Cherokee account, all the animals were originally in *galúnlati*, the world above the sky vault, which is made of solid rock. Beneath, there was nothing but water.

Since the animals were crowded in *galúnlati*, they wondered if there could be anything under the water. At last the water beetle, called Beaver's Grandchild, offered to go find out. It dived to the bottom and came up with soft mud, which grew until it formed the island we call earth. . . .

The sun's preeminence in Southeast lore is unmistakable, especially in the older traditions. Often as not, and perhaps typically, the sun was a woman.[6]

5

BUFFALO HUSBAND

NORTHERN PLAINS
(BLACKFEET)

INTRODUCTION

Long ago, the Blackfeet people followed the buffalo over a vast area of the northern plains that includes present-day Montana and southern Canada. Broad prairies, interrupted by minor mountain ranges, green river valleys, and deep ravines attracted huge herds of buffalo. The Blackfeet people depended on buffalo for meat; for hides to cover their tipis, and to make into shirts, robes, leggings, moccasins, and bedding; for bones to make into knives, awls, scrapers, and other weapons and tools; and for horns to make into bowls and spoons. But hunting buffalo was a difficult and dangerous task.

Before horses came to the Great Plains, hunters followed the great herds on foot. But because buffalo traveled too fast to be chased, hunters had to dream up ways to outsmart them. One of these inventions was a V-shaped corral called a *pis'kun* designed by the Blackfeet to force buffalo herds to run over the edges of tall cliffs. Blackfeet hunters would drive two tall poles into the ground a short distance apart at the very edge of a cliff creating an open point, or bottom, of the V. From there, the hunters fanned out two rows of poles across the prairie to form the top of the V.

When the hunters learned a buffalo herd was in the area, they disguised themselves as wolves and lined up along the flared rows of the *pis'kun*. When the buffalo approached, the hunters would jump up and begin to hoot and holler. The buffalo herd would go wild and stampede toward the pointed end of the V at the edge of the cliff. After the buffalo tumbled over the edge, Blackfeet hunters would then collect the dead and wounded from the prairie below where they had landed.[1]

However, legend tells that a very long time ago the buffalo refused to be frightened by the wolves who laid in wait along the edges of the *pis'kun*, and they would not stampede to the edge of the cliff. Instead, they veered away, and fled down the cliff's sloping sides.

The origin of the buffalo dance, as told in the story of "Buffalo Husband," explains how the Blackfeet people learned to keep the buffalo tumbling off the cliff and the tribe from starving.[2]

Buffalo Husband

≪◆X◆X◆X◆X◆X◆≫≺◆X◆X◆X◆X◆X◆≻≺◆X◆X◆X◆X◆X◆≫

One morning when the prairie grass glistened with early frost, a young Blackfeet woman got up and slipped quietly out of her tipi. She was on her way to the stream when a small pebble dropped from the sky. Surprised, the young woman looked up. There high above her on the edge of the nearby cliff was a great herd of buffalo, the first to appear since spring.

"Jump," she called to them. "Jump. Please jump. Our people are very hungry." But the buffalo just paced back and forth along the cliff's edge. Finally, in desperation, the young woman called out to them, "If you jump, I will marry one of you."

A huge cloud of dust rose above the cliff as the heavy animals pushed and shoved one another to position themselves. Then they began to tumble over the edge, and their giant bodies rained down onto the prairie below.

The young woman was so happy she could hardly contain herself. She turned to run home with the good news. But before she could take a step, a huge buffalo bull charged toward her.

The young woman shook with fear. "No, no," she exclaimed. "I did not really mean what I said. I cannot marry a buffalo."

The buffalo bull grabbed her by the arm. "Look at all of my dead and wounded brothers," he said. "We have saved your people from starvation. You must honor your promise to marry." And he began to drag the young woman off across the prairie.

It was not until sometime after all the buffalo had been slaughtered that the young woman was missed by her family.

"My beautiful daughter is gone," said an old man. "I must find her."

The people protested. "You cannot go after the herd. You will be trampled."

But the old man took up his bow and arrows and headed off across the prairie. He walked for many hours. But there were no buffalo in sight. Discouraged and tired, the old man sat down to rest beside a small stream. Overhead a spirited young magpie flew back and forth. Back and forth. He flashed the bright patches of white on his short rounded wings.

"Please, clever bird," said the old man. "Find my daughter and tell her where I wait." The magpie flicked his wedge-shaped tail at the old man and flew away.

Magpies always know where buffalo herds graze, and this young one had no trouble finding the old man's daughter. When the magpie saw where the young woman rested near her buffalo husband, he flew down beside her and whispered in her ear, "Your father waits for you by the stream. He will take you home."

The young woman shook with fright. "My buffalo husband sleeps. If he wakes and sees you here I will be punished. Go and tell my father to wait for me. I will come when it is safe."

As the magpie flew off, Buffalo Husband woke up. "I am thirsty," he growled. "Go to the stream and fetch me water."

Eager to see her father, the young woman hurried off to fill her husband's cup with water.

When she came to the stream she saw her father patiently waiting.

"Father. Why have you come here?" she asked him. "Buffalo Husband will kill you if he finds you."

"I came to take you home," her father said. And he took his daughter gently by the arm.

"No. No," said the daughter. "It is not good. The herd will chase us and kill us. I must wait until Buffalo Husband sleeps again. Then I will return."

Tears flowed from the old man's eyes as he watched his beautiful young daughter return to the herd.

The young woman drew her robe tightly around her slumped shoulders and walked slowly back to her buffalo husband. She could not think of a way to escape. When she returned home, Buffalo Husband grabbed the water from her hand and drank it down. Then his eyes narrowed and his great nostrils widened.

"A person is close by here," he said, rising slowly onto his hind quarters. He tossed his shaggy head backward and gave a great buffalo bellow. The herd awoke, rose up, and bellowed back. Then the bulls dropped their heads to the ground, rutted around in the dirt, and stampeded off to the stream.

It did not take long for the herd to find the young woman's father. And it took even less time for them to trample the poor old man into the ground. When they were sure his body was finely ground up in the mud, they cocked their heads in the air and headed home.

The young woman knew when the herd returned that her dear father was dead. "You have killed my father," she cried at Buffalo Husband. "Why? He did not harm you."

"I feel no pity," growled Buffalo Husband. "You ran our

mothers, fathers, and children off the cliff. You slaughtered them for food, and we too mourned. I have no pity."

The young woman fell to the ground sobbing. "My dear father. My dear father," she lamented. "What have I done?"

Buffalo Husband's eyes softened. He slumped down beside her and pressed his great warm body against her limp one. "I will give you another chance," he muttered. "If you can bring your father back to life, I will let both of you go home to your people."

The young woman looked into the eyes of Buffalo Husband. She knew he would keep his promise. But she did not know how she could possibly bring her father back to life.

Then she heard the loud caw caw of the magpie overhead. "Please," she said to the spirited young bird, "go to the banks of the stream; look in the mud for a piece of my father, and bring it to me."

Always quick to respond to a challenge, the magpie flew off toward the stream. He poked his thick pointed beak into the mud like he was looking for grasshoppers or crickets in the prairie grass. Before long something hard and white turned up. The magpie plucked it up and rubbed it against his shiny iridescent feathers. When all the mud was gone, a small white piece of vertebra appeared. It was a bone from the spine of the young woman's father.

The magpie took the piece of bone and flew off. When he gave it to the young woman she cradled it in her thin white hands. "I will make you whole again, dear father," she whispered into her palms.

The young woman placed her father's bone on the ground, slipped her long robe off her shoulders, and covered the little vertebra. Then she began to sing a long mournful song. When the song ended she lifted the edge

of her robe and peered beneath it. There lay her beloved father. Whole. But without life.

The young woman covered the entire body again and began to sing another song. This time she sang a song so joyful even the mountain birds came to listen. When she finished, she lifted the edge of the robe and peered beneath it. Her father smiled up at her. Then he rose slowly to his feet.

"Your people medicine is very strong," said Buffalo Husband. "Even after we trampled your father to death he is alive again. These are strange events for us to see."

The buffalo herd bellowed in disbelief. The magpie flew around in foolish circles. And the young woman jumped with joy.

Buffalo Husband paced back and forth, thinking, in front of the young woman and her father. Finally he said, "I will free you as I promised. But first you must learn buffalo medicine."

He called his bulls to form a great even circle around him, and Buffalo Husband signaled them to dance. Then he began to sing. Wind carried his sacred song far out over the prairie while the earth echoed the dull thump of the bulls' heavy hooves.

When the dance ended, Buffalo Husband told the young woman and her father to go home and teach the song and dance to their people. "The objects that will make our medicine work," he said, "are the bull's head and robe, which must always be worn by those who perform the dance. If you do this before and after every hunt," he added, "it will bring us back to life, and we will give ourselves to you willingly."

The young woman and her father kept their promise. And that was the beginning of *I-kun-uh'kah-tsi*, the sacred buffalo dance of the Blackfeet people.

QUESTIONS AND ANSWERS

Q: Why does the young woman promise to marry a buffalo bull?

A: She is willing to give herself in exchange for food for her people, who are starving.

Q: What part does the clever magpie play in this story?

A: The magpie is the messenger. He communicates between the young woman and her father. He is also the one who finds and returns the old man's bone to his daughter so she can bring him back to life.

Q: Why is the buffalo dance important in the relationship between the Blackfeet and the buffalo?

A: The buffalo dance honors the buffalo and allows them to give themselves willingly to the Blackfeet people. It insures that the buffalo will be restored to life.

Q: What medicine objects are important to wear in the buffalo dance?

A: The bull's head and robe. By mimicking the buffalo, the dancers are showing their respect for the animals.

Q: Why is it important that Blackfeet hunters honor the buffalo?

A: If the buffalo are not appeased, they will be offended and might not return. Then the people will starve to death. Appeasing them with the ritual buffalo dance honors them. It is like thanking a friend for cooperating in a mutual relationship.

EXPERT COMMENTARY

In *The Power of Myth*, Joseph Campbell, a noted scholar of mythology, author, and lecturer, talked with Bill Moyers, a television journalist, about the need for hunting rituals among Native Americans and other early hunters:

> Man lives by killing and there is a sense of guilt connected with that. . . .You see, the basic hunting myth is of a kind of covenant [agreement] between the animal world and the human world. The animal gives its life willingly, with the understanding that its life transcends its physical entity and will be returned to the soil or to the mother through some ritual of restoration.[3]

> . . . You find among hunting people all over the world a very intimate, appreciative relationship to the principal food animal. Now when we sit down to a meal, we thank God for giving us the food. These people thanked the animal.[4]

> . . . And sometimes the animal becomes the giver of a ritual, as in the legends of the origins of the buffalo. For example, you can see this equality in the basic legend of the Blackfoot tribe, which is the origin legend of their buffalo dance rituals by which they invoke the cooperation of the animals in this play of life.[5]

Tom McHugh, a well known zoologist and wildlife photographer, wrote in his book *The Time of the Buffalo*:

> Several folktales stressed the closeness between buffalo and Indian with tales of marriage between the two. Tribesmen believed recital of these stories would cause the herds to approach and offer themselves for slaughter.[6]

6

WINTER-MAN'S FURY

SOUTHERN PLAINS
(CHEYENNES)

INTRODUCTION

More than three hundred years ago, the Cheyennes migrated from an area around the Great Lakes to present-day North and South Dakota. Around that time, they gave up a life of farming to become expert horsemen and buffalo hunters.

Their new homeland was a vast, dry grassland in the high portion of the Great Plains. It was an area almost devoid of trees except in the mountain foothills and along rivers and streams. Wind in the region is known to blow harder and stronger than anywhere else in the United States, except along the coasts.[1]

In the beginning, before horses came to the region, the Cheyennes hunted on foot. They used dogs to pull their supplies on a small *travois*, a sledlike cart with no wheels. It was made by tying two poles together in the shape of a V. The closed end of the V was attached to the dog's shoulders, and the open end rested on the ground. A strong buffalo hide was stretched between the two poles; it held supplies above the animal's back. In the late 1700s, a similar device was made for horses.[2]

In summer, families left their winter campsites, where they had lived apart from the larger group all season, and gathered on the plains to organize communal buffalo hunts. The thick short grasses of the region attracted herds of buffalo, deer, elk, and antelope.

The Cheyennes tell a story about Winter-Man and Bow-in-Hand, two named spirit-beings who possess human personality traits. Bow-in-Hand saves his people from Winter-Man's fury after the last glacier retreated north from the Great Plains.[3]

WINTER-MAN'S FURY

Long ago, when big winters stayed on the southern plains most of the year, Air was always restless. Wind, Rain, Sun, and Snow were supposed to take turns visiting the Cheyennes. But Snow bullied everyone and took up more than his share of time.

Wind, when it got over the top of the great Rocky Mountains, was so pleased to be free that it whirled across the prairie and made the stout little grasses blow dizzily back and forth. Sometimes Wind blew hard and cold. Other times it blew soft and warm. Gentle or fierce, Wind stayed around as long as it could. Rain, on the other hand, came only in summer. It stayed until the tightly bundled roots of prairie grasses came alive. Then it headed eastward. And Sun appeared.

Sun stood high in the sky warming the prairie grasses and making them grow thick and green. It stayed until the animals who came to graze grew round and plump. Then it made way for Ho-e-ma-ha, the Winter-Man, who nipped at its heels and often refused to wait his turn.

By September, Winter-Man was already hiding under the shade of a tree during the day, but he came out only at night. In October, he walked boldly across the hilltops and onto the grassland, coming closer and closer to the Cheyenne people.

Winter-Man could not be trusted, so the Cheyennes always prepared themselves for a terrible winter. When Winter-Man was in a good mood, meat supplies lasted until he went away. But if he was in a bad mood, the people grew hungry long before he left.

Running Fast, a young Cheyenne boy, kept watch for signs of Ho-e-ma-ha. "Look," said Running Fast to his grandfather one day, "Winter-Man's moccasins have touched the earth. The grasses have turned brown."

"I see," said Grandfather. "And he is breathing on the trees. The leaves have turned yellow and are falling."

The birds tucked in their wings, flattened their feathers, and flew south; bears curled up in rotten logs and hibernated; wolves, foxes, and other small animals took refuge in rock caves; and deer, elk, and antelope nestled into deep ravines trying to stay warm. The buffalo just turned their backs and began a slow amble southward.

While everyone was scurrying around, Ho-e-ma-ha picked up his magic flute and began to play a high-pitched dissonant tune. Soon sleet and icy winds blew down on the grassy plains.

The Cheyennes took refuge in their large warm tipis. "I think Winter-Man is very angry," said Running Fast. "He has returned without warning."

Winter-Man had only begun to show his power. He stood up, shook out his powerful great long robe, and snow followed. For two long moons the Cheyennes stayed in their tipis while Winter-Man deluged them with snow and sleet. "It is good that we have stored much buffalo meat," said Running Fast's grandfather. "Or else we would die of starvation."

Winter-Man waited on the ridge above the Cheyennes'

camp expecting an elder to come out and beg for mercy. When no one appeared, he became furious and made the storm even worse. He sought out holes in the tipi covers and blew fiercely into every opening he could find. He even hovered above the very top of each tipi where the smoke escapes and blew straight down so billows of smoke filled the inside.

"Winter-Man has never been so angry," said Running Fast's grandfather. "Our buffalo meat is almost gone. Someone must go out and hunt."

Three young braves volunteered. They wrapped themselves in heavy buffalo-skin robes, took up their strong bows, and slung round oblong-shaped quivers that held extra arrows over their shoulders. Winter-Man watched with a twinkle in his eye. He had gleefully coated the snow with a thin layer of hard ice to cover the animal tracks and to make walking difficult for the hunters.

In these freezing conditions, the three young braves soon had to admit defeat, and they returned home empty-handed. In the meantime, Grandfather's youngest son, Bow-in-Hand, returned home from a trip he had taken with a neighboring tribe.

"Things are very bad, Bow-in-Hand," said his father. "Winter-Man is very angry. His furious storm is almost two moons old, and we are running out of food. Our people are starving, and we can do nothing."

"I will go and see him," said Bow-in-Hand. "Where does he make his camp?"

"He is over the ridge to the north," said his father. "But it will do no good. We cannot make him go away."

For many years the Cheyennes had feared Ho-e-ma-ha because he held the whole land in his power. They did not believe that the magic eagle-feather fan, which Bow-in-Hand kept for his people, was powerful enough to stop

Winter-Man. But Bow-in-Hand believed it held the power of Eagle-spirit. Eagle-spirit had often helped to bring the buffalo to Cheyenne country and had guided the people in battle. Bow-in-Hand was willing to test the fan made from the eagle's feathers against Winter-Man's noisy flute and great long robe.

"Look what he has done to our young braves," said Bow-in-Hand as he helped to carry the half-frozen young hunters into his father's tipi. "I must try to stop him, or we will all die."

"Then you must dress warmly. Here, take these," said his father, handing Bow-in-Hand a stack of warm buffalo hides. But Bow-in-Hand merely waved the magic

eagle-feather fan back and forth in the air to remind the old man of its power.

"Perhaps," said his father. "Perhaps."

Then Bow-in-Hand headed off to confront Winter-Man without taking any of the buffalo-skin robes offered to him by his father.

When Winter-Man saw Bow-in-Hand coming toward the ridge, he blew heavy drifts of snow into his path. Bow-in-Hand stepped lightly through the drifts and kept on walking. Then Winter-Man pelted him with sharp arrows of sleet. Still Bow-in-Hand walked on. When he reached Winter-Man's large tipi, he did not announce himself but,

instead, opened the door and went inside. Bow-in-Hand's boldness infuriated Winter-Man.

"How dare you come in here uninvited," he snarled, although he himself had never waited for an invitation to visit Cheyenne country. Then to frighten the bold intruder, Winter-Man shook his robe until the tipi was filled with snow. When Bow-in-Hand refused to respond to this gesture, Winter-Man shot arrows of sleet at close range.

Again, Bow-in-Hand did not flinch. Instead, he waved his eagle-feather fan in Winter-Man's face. As the fan moved back and forth, the snow began to melt. And the sleet turned to gentle drops of water.

"You cannot do this," said Winter-Man. "My magic flute and robe have much more power than that feeble eagle-feather fan you carry."

Then Winter-Man shuffled his great body around the tipi and looked at the walls as they melted away. He shot an icy stare at Bow-in-Hand, lifted his magic flute to his mouth, and blew loud angry noises instead of notes.

The snow continued to fall, but as it fell it melted. And the sleet turned to rain.

Winter-Man's great frosty eyes narrowed as he stared at the weightless eagle-feather fan Bow-in-Hand waved in front of him. Then Winter-Man took off his great robe and shook it with all of his might. More snow filled the tipi. But it, too, quickly melted.

At last it grew so warm inside the tipi that Winter-Man's children ran outside and hid in the cracks and fissures of the rocks. Defeated, Winter-Man stormed out the door and headed north.

When Bow-in-Hand returned home, he told his people that Winter-Man was gone forever. But he warned them that Winter-Man's children had not gone away with him and remained behind, hiding out in the crevices of rocks. "We must find them and send them away, too," Bow-in-Hand warned his people.

So the people filled large buffalo-skin bags with hot water and poured it into the cracks and crannies of rocks all over Cheyenne country. Nevertheless, many of Winter-Man's children squirmed deep down between the cracks where the water could not flow.

Winter-Man never again returned to Cheyenne country. But his children still take their turns each year to bring kinder, gentler winters to the southern plains.

QUESTIONS AND ANSWERS

Q: What is the role of Winter-Man, and what objects help him accomplish his job?

A: Winter-Man brings cold weather to the southern plains. He uses a magic flute and robe to bring snow, sleet, and ice.

Q: What were the consequences of Winter-Man's fits of anger?

A: Winter-Man was creating frigid, arctic-like conditions on the plains in which the Cheyenne people might not be able to survive.

Q: What does Bow-in-Hand use to save his people from starvation?

A: He uses his magic eagle-feather fan, which has greater power than Winter-Man's flute and robe.

Q: What is the symbolism of the eagle-feather fan?

A: Among many tribes of the Great Plains, the eagle spirit was credited with success in hunting and war. Thus eagle feathers were greatly revered, and Bow-in-Hand's eagle-feather fan held great powers.

Q: Why does winter still come to the plains, even though Winter-Man was driven away?

A: Winter-Man's children hid in the cracks of rocks and stayed behind on the plains, creating more moderate winters. Thereafter, a natural cycle of summer and winter was established.

Q: How is Bow-in-Hand a heroic figure?

A: He saved his people from Winter-Man's fury by driving him out of the plains, forever.

EXPERT COMMENTARY

E. Adamson Hoebel did field work among the Northern Cheyennes in the early part of this century and was a professor of anthropology at the University of Minnesota. His book *The Cheyennes* is a well-rounded case study that includes some of their world views. He explains:

> . . . the Cheyenne view [is] that the universe is essentially a mechanical system which is good in essence, but which must be properly understood and used to keep it producing what man needs and wants. The great spirits understand the nature of its working; they know the techniques that help it to produce. This knowledge they willingly share with mankind, if mankind seeks and listens respectfully.[4]

In his book *Astoria*, Washington Irving tells the story of John Jacob Astor's two expeditions to the mouth of the Columbia River in 1810. Astor, who planned to establish a vast empire based on the trading of furs, met hundreds of Indian tribes along the way. Expedition journals of the trip included many descriptions of Cheyenne country, including the following:

> . . . inhabitants of plains are prone to clothe the mountains that bound their horizon with fanciful and superstitious attributes. Thus the wandering tribes of the prairies, who often behold clouds gathering round the summits of these hills, and lightning flashing, and thunder pealing from them, when all the neighboring plains are serene and sunny, consider them the abode of the genii or thunderspirits who fabricate storms and tempests.[5]

7

THE KACHINAS
ARE COMING

SOUTHWEST (HOPI)

INTRODUCTION

For thousands of years the Hopi have lived on the tops of three mesas, or flat-topped tablelands, in present-day Arizona. Their multistory adobe houses share space with dry grasses, rabbit-bush, and stunted juniper and piñon trees. Below the mesas, Hopi farmers once coaxed corn, beans, and squash out of the dry sandy soil. Cultivated crops sustained the people, and fresh rabbit meat supplemented their diet.

Today, the Hopi live like many other Americans, and gardening and hunting are leisurely activities. But traditional life remains strong. The Hopi are one of the few American Indian groups who did not adopt Christianity and did not give up their religious beliefs. Thus, much of the Hopi Way remains intact today.

In ancient times, the Hopi left the Underworld along with the Kachinas, who are generous spirit-beings, and together they roamed the earth. The Kachinas danced for the Hopi and brought rain and prosperity, but eventually they returned home. Still, the Hopi call the Kachinas back each year during the winter solstice and ask them to bring rain, change the weather, help in everyday activities, punish offenders of ceremonial or social laws, and in general act as a link between gods and mortals.

During the annual winter solstice celebration, the only time during the year that Hopi clansmen impersonate Kachinas, men wear masks and dress in the costume of their chosen Kachina. They sing and dance to bring rain and answer special requests. There are hundreds of different Kachinas to impersonate, but each Hopi clan chooses only a few to be represented each year.

The rituals associated with this time of the year are

taken very seriously and must be performed correctly in order to bring the required results.

Hopi Kachinas are also represented by small wooden statuettes, or dolls, carved in imitation of particular spirit-beings. These small spirit-beings, also called Kachinas, are neither religious ornaments nor playthings. They are made to help children remember the costumes of the different Kachina spirits, and to spark their memories of the songs and dances that belong to each one.[1]

Tihkuyi, Creator of Game Animals; Masou, He Who Appears Anywhere; and Nuvak, the Snow Maiden, are important Kachinas, or spirit-beings, who are often represented during winter solstice celebrations.[2]

THE KACHINAS ARE COMING

When the world was still new, before large game animals had come to the Hopi people, mice were the only source of meat. But trapping mice took a great deal of time and patience and wound up providing very little meat for the trappers' efforts.

Shilko, the cleverest young fellow in his group, was always coming up with new ways to trick mice. "It is time to go trapping," he said, and he walked among his friends waving a small stick with a string attached.

"What does Shilko plan for today?" asked one of the boys as he eyed Shilko's stick.

"I am going to prop up a rock with this stick and put cornmeal under it," he answered. "Then, when a mouse comes to get the cornmeal, I will pull the string and the rock will fall on him."

The boys followed Shilko until he came to a spot that looked just right. They watched as he set his clever trap, stepped back to admire it, and sat down to wait.

The boys remained very quiet for a long time. No mice came to the trap. The boys waited and waited. Shilko seldom failed at anything he did. But when the sun finally came to rest on the horizon, Shilko hung his head and said,

"My trap was not so clever. We have not caught a single mouse today."

The youngest boy picked up a sack of corn and said, "I am hungry. It is time to eat." The boys built a large fire and ate heartily.

"Tonight we must throw corncobs on the fire and call the spirits in the way of our people," said Shilko. "We cannot go home empty-handed."

Shilko stood up and threw the first corncob into the fire. Each boy followed with one of his own. In a few minutes the night air was filled with clouds of billowing grey smoke. The smallest boy moved close to the fire and stood where the smoke blew in his face. "Someone please help us," he said, his voice quivering.

They waited quietly for a long time, but they heard only the crackling of the fire. At last Shilko filled the little smoking pipe his father had given him and passed it around the circle for the other boys to smoke. Then he added more cobs to the fire.

Suddenly, without warning, a tall and striking young woman appeared out of the darkness. One of the boys covered his face. Another boy ducked behind a large rock. And the two littlest ones clasped hold of each other. Everyone trembled except Shilko.

"Don't be afraid," he told the other boys. "It is Tihkuyi, our spirit-mother."

Tihkuyi's serene face and outstretched arms calmed their fears, and the boys returned to their circle formation around the fire.

"You signaled me with the smoke of your corncobs," she said. "I have come to help. Do not worry that you have no mice. They are too small for meat, anyway. I will show you how to catch larger animals."

Tihkuyi began to sing a soft haunting melody that

mingled with the curls of smoke from the fire and twisted upward into the night air. When she finished, Tihkuyi told the boys to remember the song so they could teach it to their mothers and sisters, who would sing it while they were grinding corn.

Tihkuyi sat down beside Shilko and said, "You will know when you awake in the morning if Nuvak, or Snow-Maiden, has heard my song."

"How will I know?" asked Shilko.

Tihkuyi made marks like rabbit tracks on the ground and said, "You will see footprints like this in the morning. They will belong to the rabbits. Follow the footprints to where the rabbits hide in the rocks and pull them out."

The boys were very excited about the prospect of catching animals larger than mice. Before Tihkuyi disappeared into the night, Shilko gave her a prayer-stick decorated with beautiful feathers.

The next morning, when the boys awoke, the ground was covered with snow—something they had never seen before.

"My feet are freezing," whined one of the younger boys. So Shilko tore up the corn sack they had brought from home and gave each of the boys two pieces to wrap around his feet.

Soon after they left camp, the boys found rabbit tracks in the snow just like those Tihkuyi had drawn in the sand. They followed the tracks toward a great outcropping of rock and waited quietly for the rabbits to come out of their holes. When they did, the boys smacked them with their small wooden clubs. Soon they had enough rabbits to take back to camp.

After dinner that evening, Shilko threw more corncobs on the fire and waited for Tihkuyi to reappear, so he could show her that Nuvak had indeed heard her song. When

Tihkuyi stepped out of the cloud of smoke, she was smiling. "You have done well," she said. "Cottontail rabbits have much meat." She showed the boys how to clean the rabbits and dress the skins to take home for the women to make into warm clothing. "Now," she said, "you need a spirit-father. Shilko, you must call him."

Shilko stepped forward and called into the night. "Is there anyone out there who will be our spirit-father? If so, please come out." Before long they heard a deep voice, and Masou came forward. He went over to where Tihkuyi stood and whispered in her ear. Together they began to draw the tracks of a jackrabbit on the ground.

"The next time you hunt or trap," said Masou, "go into the valley near your village and look for these tracks. Follow them to where the jackrabbits hide. When you are ready to catch larger animals, go into the valley below Far Mesa."

Before Masou disappeared, Shilko handed him a prayer-stick like the one he had given to Tihkuyi.

The next morning there was even more snow on the ground, but the boys were so eager to hunt jackrabbits that they tramped through the shin-deep snow without complaining. When they found the tracks, they followed them into the bushes and killed many more animals than they had the day before. In fact, the boys were so successful that they had to build a carrier out of tree branches to get all of the animals home.

But the heavy carrier filled with meat made the boys tired, so Shilko suggested they build a fire and rest. "We do not have far to go," he said. "Our village is close by."

No sooner had the boys started their fire when the men of the village saw the smoke and came to greet them. "You have done well," said one of the men. "We will help you carry the animals home. But first you must show us where you have been hunting."

Shilko stuck out his hand as if to hold back the men. "Not yet," he said. "We must return to the village and organize a proper hunt." The men agreed, and that evening Shilko announced the spot where the hunters should meet in the morning. He gave them the route they would take and named specific points along the way. The next day the men spread out in a great circle, and when rabbits appeared the hunters gradually closed the circle and rounded up many animals.

Before too long, Shilko grew bored with rabbit hunting and decided to hunt animals larger than cottontails and jackrabbits. "Bring heavier clubs today," he said very casually to the men. "It will bring us luck."

The following day, Shilko led the group on a long trek in the direction of Far Mesa where Masou had told them they would find larger animals. When they finally arrived at the foot of the mesa, Shilko directed the hunters to form a circle near its south side. He was about to signal the men to tighten the circle when he saw Masou standing in the center surrounded by deer and elk.

Their eyes met. Masou whispered, "Shout. Shout loudly, Shilko." Shilko did as he was told, and the deer and elk went wild. They ran around in circles. Faster. And faster. And faster. At last they grew tired and fell to the ground. That evening the hunters went home with fresh deer and elk meat.

The Hopi never had to trap mice again, and rabbit meat became an important source of nourishment. Deer and elk remained a special treat.

QUESTIONS AND ANSWERS

Q: Who is the most important character in the story and what are his traits?

A: Shilko, the leader of the young boys, is humble, brave, and confident.

Q: What leadership does Shilko undertake for his people?

A: He admits his mouse trap design is a failure, calls on the spirits for help, and teaches the men of his village how to hunt.

Q: Why did the boys throw corncobs onto the fire?

A: They had been taught by their elders that after throwing corncobs on a fire, and calling on the spirits for help, the spirits would appear.

Q: Why are Tihkuyi, Masou, and Nuvak important spirit-beings?

A: Tihkuyi and Masou taught the boys how to identify and follow the tracks of cottontail and jackrabbits, as well as deer and elk. Nuvak brought snow so that the boys could follow the tracks of the animals.

Q: How are Tihkuyi, Masou, and Nuvak symbolized in Hopi culture?

A: They are special Kachinas who appear as masked dancers during winter solstice celebrations. Their figures are often carved into small wooden statuettes.

Q: Why is the winter solstice celebration important to the Hopi people?

A: It is a special time when the Hopi ask spirit Kachinas to bring rain and help with important problems. The rituals associated with this time of year are taken very seriously and must be performed correctly in order to bring the required results.

Q: What is the difference between Kachina masked dancers who perform during winter solstice celebrations and Kachina statuettes, or dolls?

A: The Kachinas who wear masks, sing, and dance during winter solstice celebrations are members of Hopi clans. Kachina statuettes are small wooden dolls made to help children remember the costumes, songs, and dances associated with the spirit Kachinas.

Q: What do both types of Kachinas represent?

A: Both the masked dancers who are Hopi clansmen and the carved statuettes represent the Kachina spirit-beings who live in the Underworld and emerge during the winter solstice to bring the Hopi people rain and prosperity.

EXPERT COMMENTARY

Frederick J. Dockstader, a prominent scholar of Hopi culture, studied and lived among the Hopi people for many years. His collection of Kachina statuettes numbers in the hundreds, and he carved some of the figures in his collection himself. While associated with the Cranbrook Institute of Science in Bloomfield Hills, Michigan, Dr. Dockstader wrote extensively about Kachinas.

> While legendary accounts describe the origin of the Kachinas as a group, individual new Kachinas are introduced from time to time. . . . A number were introduced by Hopis who had seen dances in other pueblos [villages], or even in non-pueblo areas, and some were adapted from dances presented in the village areas by visiting Indians. Some admittedly and obviously were taken over from such neighboring pueblos as Zuni, Acoma, or Jemez; and a few were taken from non-pueblo tribes such as the Navajo, Comanche, or Havasupai.[3]

Edwin Earle and Edward A. Kennard, in their book *Hopi Kachinas*, said that the Hopi are much more concerned about what the Kachinas look like and how well they perform than about their meaning:

> While any Hopi can describe in detail the costume, songs, dance steps of a great number of Kachinas he remains comfortably vague on the subject of their relations to the forces of the universe, the nature of their power, and the fate of the soul after death. . . . All ceremonies are for rain and the correct performance of numerous ritual acts brings the desired result . . . . There is no tendency to develop a unified conception of the universe, to identify specific deities of their mythology with natural forces, nor to arrange them in a hierarchal system.[4]

In his book *Old Oraibi*, Mischa Titiev had a similar comment on Hopi Kachina practices:

> The complexities of their Kachina worship are of little moment to the Hopi. They make no effort to systematize or to classify their beliefs, but are content to regard the Kachinas as a host of benevolent spirits who have the best interest of the Hopi ever at heart.[5]

8

MANDAMIN

WESTERN GREAT LAKES
(ANISHINABES)

INTRODUCTION

The Anishinabes, or Chippewa/Ojibway, as they prefer to be called, were once the most powerful tribe to occupy territory around the western Great Lakes. They fished and collected wild rice in freshwater lakes and streams, and hunted in the dense woodlands of the region. Even though the planting season is relatively short in the northern woodlands, the Anishinabes raised ample quantities of corn, beans, squash, and pumpkins.

In the past, large dome-shaped wigwams each sheltered as many as eight families at a time. Hunters traveled on snowshoes in winter and paddled durable elm-bark canoes along the edges of lakes and streams while gathering wild rice in the fall.[1]

The spiritual life of the Anishinabes is as strong today as it was before corn came to the people in 200 A.D.[2] Their spirit-leader, Kitche Manitou, Maker of Life, gave order to the world and is most often represented as the sun—an eternal circle that goes around and around without beginning or end. In drawings on bark scrolls, four projections extend from the sun, each one symbolizing Kitche Manitou's presence in all places and at all times.

Mandamin, an Algonquian word meaning "food of wonder," or "corn," is the title of a story about a stranger who visits the Anishinabe people. Like the stranger named Mandamin, corn was also a stranger to the region at the time. The story is about how corn came to the Anishinabe people. More importantly, and on a more symbolic level, it is a tale about the continuity of life.[3]

MANDAMIN

A long time ago, a young boy called Zhowmin lost his parents and went to live with his grandmother, Zhaw-b'noh-quae. Grandmother taught him the ways of his people and how to be respectful, curious, and kind. Zhowmin's uncle taught him practical knowledge, like how to hunt and fish like a man.

By the time Zhowmin reached manhood he was already caring for his aged grandmother. He kept her well fed with fresh deer, antelope, and elk meat. And she kept him well clothed in animal-hide shirts and leggings.

In the evening, Grandmother told Zhowmin the tales of their people. Even when her voice grew weak and she dozed between stories, she continued to fill her grandson with the wisdom of their elders. One evening, she told him the story of the Four Hills of Life. Grandmother pointed out that each hill required each climber to have strength and endurance to reach the top and that many people never succeeded in reaching this goal. Grandmother smiled when she told Zhowmin that she had already climbed the hills of infancy, youth, and adulthood, and was ready to climb the last and final one. "Soon after I leave," she said to her grandson, "a stranger will come to you. Be sure to do what he says."

Slowly the moons came and went, one after another, and Grandmother did not leave the wigwam. Then one warm spring morning Grandmother did not answer when Zhowmin called to her. When he brought fresh stew to her bedside, she did not move. Her journey over the last of the four hills was complete.

The people of the village, saddened by the death of a woman they loved, buried Zhaw-b'noh-quae beneath a clump of young pine trees, facing west, or toward the place they called Man's Last Destiny.

Then, only a few days later, a surly young man arrived in the village. "Is there at least one good man in this village?" asked the stranger. The elders thought. Finally one of them said, "Yes, Zhowmin is a good man. We will take you to him."

Zhowmin took the stranger into his wigwam and served him a large bowl of deer stew. After they had finished eating, Zhowmin asked, "Why have you come?"

"I have traveled a long time among your people looking for a good man and have yet to find one. I understand from your elders that you are such a man."

Suddenly Zhowmin became angry. "Who are you, anyway? I certainly do not need to prove anything to a complete stranger."

The visitor straightened himself. "I will tell you who I am and why I have come. Then you will listen."

Zhowmin remained silent.

"I am Mandamin. I was sent by Kitche Manitou, Maker of Life, to find a good man and to test his inner strength. But first that man must fight with me. If you win, you will have proven the worth of your people and you will live. If you lose, you will die."

Zhowmin did not believe that Mandamin was a messenger of Kitche Manitou so he protested again. "I do not have to prove myself to you or anyone else."

"It is true you do not have to," said Mandamin. "But I will interpret your refusal to fight as cowardice, which is the same as defeat. And I will report to Kitche Manitou that I have not found a single worthy man among the Anishinabe people."

Zhowmin grew very angry. He did not care what the stranger thought of his courage, but he did not want Kitche Manitou to think that the Anishinabe people were unworthy.

Then Zhowmin remembered that his grandmother had warned him that a stranger would visit and he must do as he was told. "All right," Zhowmin agreed at last. "I will fight to prove my people worthy."

That night Mandamin and Zhowmin met in a clearing in the forest. They stripped to the waist, postured themselves in the center of the clearing, and began to circle. Equal in size and strength, the men twisted each other's limbs, punched, hit and poked each other all over. But neither man fell to the ground. At last they became bored. "Let's quit for tonight," suggested Mandamin. Zhowmin agreed, and they dragged their bruised bodies back to the wigwam, dropped onto the thick deerskin mats, and fell asleep.

During the night Mandamin grew hungry. "Is there anything to eat?" he asked. Zhowmin got up, lit the fire, and heated some stew. Then the two men sat together and ate as if they were the best of friends. When they finished eating they sat in silence together.

Finally Zhowmin spoke, "It is time to fight again." And they headed back to the forest. This time the two men fought so violently they uprooted trees and made the tall grasses disappear. Zhowmin threw Mandamin on the ground. But Mandamin got up and punched him back. They did this for a long time, until both men finally grew bored and agreed to go home again and rest.

The next day, however, Zhowmin was determined to put an end to the fighting. "I am tired of this," he said to Mandamin. "Today I will win because I do not want to die."

Mandamin raised his eyebrows and smirked. "Today, I will win," he retorted. For the first time since the fighting began the men fought like mortal enemies. They punched, kicked, and twisted. First one went down, then the other. The battle appeared to be no more decisive than the previous two fights, until finally Zhowmin struck Mandamin so hard he fell to the ground and did not get up again. Mandamin's limp body lay motionless on the ground. When Zhowmin realized he had killed the stranger, he knelt down beside him and wept.

At last Zhowmin picked up Mandamin, carried him to the clump of pine trees, and buried him beside Zhawb'noh-quae, his beloved grandmother.

The pain of having killed a man was so great that Zhowmin took his story to a medicine man. "Your grandmother made you promise to do as you were told," said the wise old medicine man. "And you have done right. Now you must take care of both their graves."

Zhowmin kept the graves weeded and well-watered until one day a small green plant emerged from the soil in the center of Mandamin's grave. Zhowmin had never seen such tough little leaves and asked the medicine man to come and take a look.

"I have never seen a plant like this," said the medicine man. He smelled it. And felt it. Then he patted the soil around the base of the little plant and said, "You must keep

it watered. We will wait until it grows up to see what it becomes."

Zhowmin tended the little plant every day. By early summer the leaves grew up to his knees. And by late summer a feathery brown tassel on the top of the plant blew high above his head.

"Come," said Zhowmin to the medicine man. "See how tall the little plant has grown." The medicine man stroked the long thick leaves of the plant and brushed his fingers against the fuzzy brown tassel. "It is good," he said. Then he opened one of the fat green husks along the stalk and plucked a small yellow seed kernel from inside. He popped it into his mouth and smacked his lips. "It is nice and sweet," he said to Zhowmin. "Taste it."

Zhowmin knew at once that the spirit of the plant had given itself to the medicine man. "Yes," he said as he tasted one of the little seeds. "It is very good."

"The plant is corn, food of wonder," said the medicine man. "It is our gift from Kitche Manitou because you have proven yourself and our people worthy of his great gift. By his death, Mandamin has given nourishment to the Anishinabe people. You have not killed him, you have merely given him life in a new form."

QUESTIONS AND ANSWERS

Q: Why is the stranger named Mandamin?

A: The word *Mandamin* in the Algonquian language means "food of wonder," or "corn," which, like Mandamin, was a stranger to the region.

Q: What are the Four Hills of Life?

A: The Anishinabes believe there are four stages in life, each one a more difficult climb than the former: infancy, youth, adulthood, and death. During her climb to the top of the last hill, Grandmother worked hard to pass on to her grandson all the wisdom she had accumulated in a lifetime of climbing the hills.

Q: What lessons did Zhowmin learn from his grandmother?

A: He learned the importance of human conduct and character. Even though he did not want to fight, he did so to save his people from Kitche Manitou's scorn.

Q: What does corn symbolize in this story?

A: It symbolizes the continuation of life in a new form in the real world after death.

Q: Why is corn used as an example of renewal?

A: Corn must be tended and nourished in order to grow and reproduce. Its seeds may be used to grow new plants, starting new life every year.

Q: Who is Kitche Manitou and what is his symbol?

A: Kitche Manitou is the spirit-leader, or creator, of the Anishinabe people. His symbol is an eternal circle in the form of the sun with four projections extending out in four directions. Each projection symbolizes Kitche Manitou's presence in all places and at all times.

EXPERT COMMENTARY

Basil Johnston lives on the Cape Croker Indian reserve in Ontario, Canada. He teaches his people their language, history, and mythology. He has written extensively, and currently works in the Department of Ethnology at the Royal Ontario Museum in Toronto. He says:

> If the Native Peoples and their heritage are to be understood, it is their beliefs, insights, concepts, ideals, values, attitudes, and codes that must be studied. . . . As it is in story, fable, legend, and myth that fundamental understandings, insights, and attitudes toward life and human conduct, character, and quality in their diverse forms are embodied and passed on. . . .

> But the story is not really about corn or its origins. It bears several themes. One of the themes is the continuation of life in a new form in the Land of the Living after death.[4]

Edmund Jefferson Danziger Jr., professor of history at Bowling Green State University, wrote in his book *The Chippewas of Lake Superior*:

> Like religious thought and practice, folklore was interwoven into the fabric of traditional Chippewa culture, revealing much about the attitudes toward life and the manidog (manitou). Storytellers used folk history to emphasize such religious and ethical values as courage, daring, and right action—not just to entertain children and adults on long winter nights.[5]

Joseph Campbell said of the Ojibway legend of the origin of corn:

> Of special interest in the Ojibwa legend . . . are two details: the appearance of the visionary messenger in human form, and the nature of the bestowed boon [gift], not as a gift simply of personal power and protection, but as a transformation of the very body of the messenger himself.[6]

9

GLOOSCAP THE TEACHER

EASTERN WOODLANDS
(MICMACS)

INTRODUCTION

During the sixteenth century, bands of the Micmacs lived in Canada, occupying the region south and west of the Gulf of St. Lawrence, which included the Maritime provinces and the Gaspe Peninsula. Winters in the region were long and cold, and summers were too short to cultivate crops. Yet the dense forests of the region attracted herds of moose, elk, and caribou, and the plentiful rivers of the north nourished schools of spawning herring, sturgeon, and salmon, which kept the people well fed all year long.

The Micmacs traveled in small groups and set up seasonal camps according to each of the "moons," or lunar phases, which were characterized by the principal kind of fish or game available. From "frost-fish or tomcod" in January to "young seals or get herring" in May, the Micmacs fished and hunted seals and otters along the rocky northeastern coast, and hunted moose, bears, and beavers inland. Summer was spent along the coastline, where men caught codfish and women gathered shellfish until the middle of September.[1]

The Micmacs were loosely organized into bands that came together during the summer. The eldest son of a powerful family often became a band's leader, or sagamore. Sagamores controlled specific fishing and hunting territories, and they exchanged gifts with each other to smooth over any disputes. They held council meetings during the summer to discuss the signing of treaties for the common good of all the people.

Families lived in conical-shaped wigwams that were framed with young sapling trees and covered with birch-bark or woven mats. The floors of the interiors were covered with fresh evergreen boughs and blanketed with thick bearskin rugs.

The Micmacs handled animal bones with great respect. They believed that the bones of animals could transform themselves, along with their entire species, into the type of animal that had eaten or absorbed the bones. Thus, beaver bones were never given to dogs, lest the beavers develop the characteristics of the dog, nor were the bones discarded in rivers, since the beavers might come to resemble some kind of fish.

Glooscap, the legendary hero of the Micmacs and their neighbors, the Maliseet-Passamaquoddy and the Abenaki, was a trickster-transformer capable of both good and evil. Even as a trickster, Glooscap was never as threatening as *puwo-win*, a male or female witch who could cause harm by making evil wishes. In the following tale, Glooscap encounters just such a witch, disguised as a young woman. He takes her aboard his magical granite canoe, but, as usual, his superior powers prevail.[2]

The story of Glooscap's journey to the world beyond, the Micmacs' version of heaven, is a story similar to the well-known Greek myth about the first woman, named Pandora. She was sent to earth by the Greek god Zeus, but before she left the gods, Zeus gave Pandora a box to take with her. Zeus instructed her never to open this box, but Pandora's curiosity finally compelled her not to listen to the gods. It was this act of disobedience that allowed all the evils in the world to escape when she opened the box.[3]

GLOOSCAP THE TEACHER

Long ago, Glooscap, the hero of the Micmac people, came to the northeast from far across the sea. He took the form of a serious and wise old man whose duty it was to teach the Micmacs all that they needed to know. Glooscap taught the people the names of all the stars and constellations and to locate them in the night sky. Eventually, the people marked their seasonal activities with names given to each of the new moons.

Glooscap also taught the people to hunt moose, elk, and caribou along the edges of the dense forests and open meadows where the animals came to feed. Men learned how to take the meat from these large animals and how to use their bones and antlers to fashion needles, awls, fishhooks, and scrapers. Glooscap showed them how to make sharp arrows and knives out of fine-grained rocks using a small piece of deer or elk antler to work the stones. "Respect the animals and use them well," said Glooscap. "They will provide you with food and material to make many tools."

After Glooscap had introduced the people to the animals of the forest, he led them to the broad rushing rivers that spilled their waters out of the mountains of the northeast. He instructed the people on how to build fish weirs, or stone nets, across the mouths of rivers to catch schools of spawning sturgeon, salmon, smelt, and herring.

To show the people he had greater power than witches, Glooscap set out to sea in a heavy granite canoe. Along the way he picked up a young woman, who was floundering in the water. "Come aboard," he said. "I will take you to shore." But no sooner was the young woman settled into the canoe than a fierce storm rose out of the sea, and great waves swept over Glooscap's heavy canoe. "You are a witch and you have done this," he said accusingly to the young woman who sat calmly in the bow of the canoe. "You are trying to drown me."

The young woman did not speak.

Glooscap paddled furiously toward shore while huge waves battered the sides of the canoe. At last he stretched his long legs toward land and planted one foot firmly on shore. When the young woman tried to follow, he held her back until he could shove the canoe far out into the sea. "Go," he said. "Become anything you desire."

Glooscap's power proved to be superior to the young witch's. Slowly she drifted out to sea and became a large ugly fish with a huge dorsal fin. Thereafter, the people knew her as *keeganibe*, the great fish.

Then, to help the Micmacs visualize life after death, Glooscap described a beautiful peaceful land far away to the west. This beautiful place was Glooscap's home, and someday it would also be the Micmacs' home, he promised the people, if they led a good life. "The journey west is long and difficult," warned Glooscap, "but the way back is short and easy."

Glooscap then described for the people the journey of seven young men who had traveled west. He listed and described the obstacles that had presented themselves along the way.

First the men had to climb a great mountain, on the tip

of which lay an overhanging cliff. To get down the other side of the mountain, the seven young men had to struggle over the edge of the cliff and descend a steep stone wall into the valley below. Fearful and distrusting men could not make the descent, but brave and honest men could accomplish it with ease.

After they climbed over the mountain, the men had to dart between the fangs of two huge serpents that guarded either side of a long narrow valley. Good men with kind hearts could slip through the serpents' fangs, but bad men with evil thoughts would be destroyed. The last obstacle in their journey was a thick dark cloud that separated the real world from the beautiful region beyond. The cloud rose and fell with no regular pattern, making it difficult to tell when it would be safe to pass underneath. Good kind men could race beneath the cloud while it was up and avoid being crushed. But evil men would be crushed into tiny bits of flesh and bone when the cloud landed on top of them. Luckily, the seven men overcame all the obstacles.

Glooscap continued his story: In the beautiful land beyond the thick dark cloud, the men visited Glooscap's wigwam, as well as the wigwams of Coolpujot and Kuhkw. Glooscap, who reigned supreme in the region, welcomed them warmly. Coolpujot, on the other hand, had no bones and could not move about. "I have him rolled over each spring and fall," explained Glooscap. "In the autumn he is turned toward the west, and in the spring he is turned toward the east. Coolpujot is responsible for the seasons: he breathes cold air and icy winds in fall, chilling frost and blowing snow in winter, pouring rain in spring, and warm yellow sunshine in summer."

Kuhkw's wigwam was large and very dark. "I call him earthquake," said Glooscap. "He travels beneath the earth kicking his feet and making the land tremble and shake. He is very powerful."

After introducing the young men to Coolpujot and Kuhkw, Glooscap gathered all seven around him, praised them for having completed their journey, and offered to grant them any wish they might desire.

At this point Glooscap paused in telling his story. He wanted to make sure the Micmacs, who were listening to the long tale, would pay special attention to the fate of the men who had made wishes. Then he continued his story:

One of the men stepped forward and asked that he be allowed to live forever and remain in this beautiful region. So Coolpujot picked up the young man and planted him firmly in the ground where he became a tall strong cedar tree. Then Coolpujot blew wind through his boughs, and fine cedar seeds flew off in all directions, creating the dense cedar groves that continue to grow plentifully throughout the northeast.

The remaining men asked that they be allowed to go home, once their wishes were granted. So Glooscap put their wishes in small packages and sent them on their way, instructing the men not to open their wish-packages until they arrived home in their various villages. Some of them made it all the way home. But two of the men failed to obey Glooscap's instructions.

One man had wished for the cure to a disease that he would not reveal, and Glooscap gave the man a small wish-package of medicine. But on his way home, the man could not help feeling the package, turning it around and around in his hand. Finally, his curiosity was too great, and he sat down to examine the parcel, then quickly opened it. Whoosh, out poured a stream of liquid onto the ground. It spread over the earth in all directions, and then it quickly disappeared. So did the man.

The second disobedient man had wished for the power to win the heart of a young woman. The young man confessed that for many years he had tried in vain to find a wife. Glooscap told him that since this was such a difficult request that he would need to confer with Coolpujot and Kuhkw. "We could never find him a wife," said Coolpujot. "He is much too ugly. And his manners are atrocious." But Glooscap was determined to make good on his promise to grant wishes to those who had succeeded in making the long journey, and he thought for a very long time. At last he went to his wigwam and returned with a sealed container. "Do not open this container until you have reached your village," Glooscap warned, as usual.

With his heart filled with hope and joy, the young man thanked Glooscap and headed home. Along the way he fantasized about the contents of his package and smiled whenever he pictured himself as handsome and charming. Then, the night before the young man was due to arrive in his village, he could wait no longer to open the magical container. Like a curious impetuous child, he stopped walking and broke open the seal.

Whoosh, out flew hundreds of beautiful women. They swarmed over his head and all around him. The young man could not believe his good fortune and became giddy with desire. But his joy was short-lived. Soon the women began to heap themselves on top of him. One after another, they stacked themselves higher and higher on top of the young man, until the weight of so many bodies finally crushed him into the ground. When the sun rose the following day, the women had vanished, and only tiny pieces of the ugly young man remained.

After Glooscap had described the adventures of the disobedient men, he reminded the Micmac people: "Each of you has much to learn before you will undertake your own journey to the beautiful land to the west. I will return another day to teach you more."

Then Glooscap the teacher hopped into his granite canoe and paddled away, rowing in a westerly direction.

QUESTIONS AND ANSWERS

Q: Were the Micmacs farmers?

A: No. They were hunters and fishermen. Winters in the northeast are long and cold, and the summer season is too short to cultivate crops.

Q: Describe Glooscap and his accomplishments.

A: Glooscap was a trickster-transformer capable of both good and evil. He was revered for the practical knowledge he gave to the people.

Q: Name three important skills Glooscap taught the people.

A: Glooscap taught the Micmacs astronomy (the names of stars and constellations); where to find elk, moose, and caribou; and how to catch spawning fish in spring.

Q: Describe Glooscap's homeland.

A: He lived in a beautiful land far away to the west. It was the last resting place of the people, or the equivalent of the Christian heaven.

Q: Name three obstacles that had to be overcome on the journey west.

A: There were high mountains with a steep overhanging cliff on top, two deadly serpents, and a great dark cloud that separated the real world from the world beyond.

Q: Who were the other mythological figures who lived in wigwams alongside Glooscap, and what natural forces did they symbolize?

A: Coolpujot represented the seasons and weather, and Kuhkw caused earthquakes.

Q: What was the reward for having made a successful journey west?

A: Glooscap would grant any wish to everyone who succeeded.

Q: How does the curiosity of the young men in Glooscap's tale resemble that of Pandora in the Greek myth?

A: Like Pandora, the men let their curiosity overcome their good judgment. Pandora was never supposed to open her box (but she did), and the men opened their packages prematurely.

EXPERT COMMENTARY

Lewis Spence, a distinguished British anthropologist and folklorist, collected many tales from the Indians of North America in the early 1900s. His book *The Myths of the North American Indians* was an early study of native myths. It includes important historical and ethnological information about a number of well-known tribes. Spence studied and retold tales from the northeast whose mythology he found to be rich and extensive.

> The Algonquin Indians [Algonkian-speaking] have perhaps a more extensive mythology than the majority of Indian peoples, and as they have been known to civilization for several centuries their myths have the advantage of having been thoroughly examined.
>
> . . . One of the most interesting figures in their pantheon is Glooskap, which means "The Liar"; but so far from an affront being intended to the deity by this appellation, it was bestowed as a compliment to his craftiness, cunning being regarded as one of the virtues by all. . . .[4]

Dr. Dean B. Bennett's book *Maine Dirigo* is a valuable teaching tool created for junior high school students in the state of Maine. The textbook includes information on the history, environment, government, and economy of the state along with chapters dealing with the Wabanakis, who share their mythology with the Micmacs of the region. In a chapter titled "Nature Is Sacred," Dr. Bennett presents a contemporary view of the people's hero, Glooskap[sic]:

> When missionaries tried to convert us, they felt they had to tell us that our Great Spirit was the devil. They also told us that our hero Glooskap was a liar! But, to us he was a mighty hero. He did wonderful things for us and taught us everything we needed to know to live in this world because he cared for us. Some say the Europeans made him go away and leave us, but it is also said that he will come again to our people.[5]

GLOSSARY

Algonquian (Al-gon-Kee-in)—The language spoken by a number of Indian tribes including the Blackfeet and Anishinabes.

camass—A native Pacific Coast wildflower that resembles a wild hyacinth. Camass plants grow in moist fields and along streams. The bulbs of camass plants formerly constituted a major portion of the plant foods of the Vancouver Indians. Bulbs are collected and stored. Later, they are either boiled, roasted, fried, or cooked with other foods.

corral—An enclosure made of wood or brush designed to trap animals.

cradleboard—A flat wooden carrier for babies made with leather sides and lacing, often lined with animal furs.

Kachina—A Hopi spirit-being who dances and brings rain during the annual winter solstice celebrations. Also, a Hopi clansman dressed as a spirit-being, or a carved statuette representing such a spirit-being.

Kitche Manitou (Maker of Life)—The cause, force, or mystical energy assumed by Algonquian-speaking tribes to be inherent in every one of nature's beings. It affects and controls the welfare of humans.

mä—A word used by the Tsimshian people to describe daylight, which was contained in a special box under the protection of the Sky Chief.

Masou (Ma-so-oo)—He Who Appears Anywhere. Masou grants both good and evil requests. In the beginning, he was a supernatural being in human form, but later he disappeared and became a spirit. He is most often depicted as a generous and kind spirit.

Nuvak—Also called Snow Maiden. The Hopi appeal to this female spirit to bring snow to the mountains so that hunters can follow the tracks of animals and the melting snow can feed fresh water streams in spring.

pis'kun—A V-shaped corral used by Blackfeet Indians designed to force buffalo herds off the edge of a cliff.

quiver—A cylindrical bark or leather arrow holder that has a long leather strap worn over the shoulder.

sagamore—The leader of a band of Micmac Indians.

solstice—The time of year when the sun is nearest or farthest from the equator. The summer solstice (about June 22) marks the beginning of summer, and the winter solstice (about December 22) marks the start of winter.

Tihkuyi (Tee-koo-yee)—A female deity, Creator of Game Animals, who gave birth to all the species of game animals, from rabbits to elk. Offerings are left at her shrine during winter solstice ceremonies so that she may increase the supply of game. Hunters must ask permission to kill her children.

tipi—A cone-shaped tent, usually made of hides stretched over wooden poles, used especially by American Indians of the plains.

travois—A sledlike cart with no wheels pulled by dogs.

tribe—A term used by nonIndians that is often applied to many different Indian social groups. A tribe usually shares a common history, culture, geographic region, and language.

wattle and daub—A method of building house walls. This method uses a frame of upright or interwoven saplings to hold mud fill and is used primarily by tribes in the southeast and southwest.

CHAPTER NOTES

Preface

1. Franz Boas, *Race, Language, and Culture*. (Chicago: The University of Chicago Press, 1940), pp. 199–201.

2. Carl Waldman, *Encyclopedia of Native American Tribes*. (New York: Facts on File Publications, 1988), pp. 240–241.

3. Ibid., p.188.

Chapter 1. Northwest (Tsimshians): Raven Steals Daylight from the Sky

1. Wayne Shuttles, volume editor. *Handbook of North American Indians*, vol. 7 (Northwest Coast). (Washington, D.C.: Smithsonian Institution, 1990), pp. 267–269.

2. Carl Waldman, *Encyclopedia of Native American Tribes*. (New York: Facts on File Publications, 1988), pp. 236–238.

3. Alonda Jonaitis. *Chiefly Feasts*. (Seattle: University of Washington Press, 1991), p. 11.

4. Adapted from texts recorded by Henry W. Tate and reported by Franz Boas in the 31st Annual Report of the Bureau of American Ethnology, 1909-1919, "Tsimshian Myths," pp. 58–62.

5. Franz Boas, *Race, Language and Culture*. (Chicago: The University of Chicago Press, 1940), p. 409.

6. Joseph Campbell, *Historical Atlas of World Mythology. Vol. I: The Way of the Animal Powers, Part 2: Mythologies of the Great Hunt*. (New York: Harper & Row, 1988), p. 186.

Chapter 2. Coast Plateau (Salish): The Moon Epic

1. Gerald S. Snyder, *In the Footsteps of Lewis and Clark*. (Washington, D.C.: National Geographic Society, 1970), p. 170.

2. Arthur C. Ballard, *Mythology of Southern Puget Sound*. (Seattle: University of Washington Press, 1929), pp. 69–80.

3. Franz Boas, *Race, Language and Culture*. (Chicago: The University of Chicago Press, 1982), p. 476.

4. John Bierhorst, *The Mythology of North America*. (New York: William Morrow and Company, 1985), p. 137.

Chapter 3. California (Maidu): Tolowim-Woman and Butterfly-Man

1. A. L. Kroeber, *Handbook of the Indians of California*. (New York: Dover Publications, Inc., 1976), p. 440.

2. Ibid., p. 439.

3. Theodora Kroeber, *The Inland Whale*. (Berkeley: University of California Press, 1959), pp. 69–73, 176.

4. A. L. Kroeber, p. 439.

5. Theodora Kroeber, p. 177.

Chapter 4. Southeast (Cherokees): How the World Was Made

1. Charles Hudson, *The Southeastern Indians*. (Knoxville: University of Tennessee Press, 1976), p. 126.

2. James Mooney, *History, Myths, and Sacred Formulas of the Cherokees*. (Asheville, N.C.: Historical Images, 1992), pp. 239–240.

3. Ibid., p. 430.

4. Hudson, p. 122.

5. Ibid., pp. 123–125.

6. John Bierhorst, *The Mythology of North America*. (New York: William Morrow and Company, 1985), pp. 1909–1912.

Chapter 5. Northern Plains (Blackfeet): Buffalo Husband

1. Tom McHugh, *The Time of the Buffalo*. (Lincoln: University of Nebraska Press, 1972), pp. 60–82.

2. George Bird Grinnell, *Blackfoot Lodge Tales*. (Williamstown, Mass.: Corner House Publications, 1972), pp. 104–107.

3. Joseph Campbell, *The Power of Myth*. (New York: Doubleday, 1988), p. 72.

4. Ibid., p. 74.

5. Ibid., p. 75.

6. McHugh, p. 136.

Chapter 6. Southern Plains (Cheyennes): Winter-Man's Fury

1. E. Adamson Hoebel, *The Cheyennes*. (New York: Holt, Rinehart and Winston, 1960), pp. 58–59.

2. Ibid., p. 65.

3. Grace Jackson Penny, *Tales of the Cheyenne*. (Boston, Mass.: Houghton Mifflin Co., 1953), pp. 44–51.

4. Hoebel, p. 83.

5. Washington Irving, *Astoria*. (Norman: University of Oklahoma Press, 1964), pp. 231–232.

Chapter 7. Southwest (Hopi): The Kachinas Are Coming

1. Jesse Walter Fewkes, *Hopi Katcinas*. (New York: Dover Publications, Inc., 1985), general reference.

2. E. S. Curtis, *The North American Indian*. (vol. XII). (New York: Johnson Reprint, 1970), pp. 190–191.

3. Frederick J. Dockstader, *The Kachina and the White Man: A Study of the Influences of White Culture on the Hopi Kachina Cult*. (Albuquerque: The University of New Mexico Press, 1985), p. 11.

4. Edwin Earle and Edward A. Kennard, *Hopi Kachinas*. (New York: J. J. Augustin, 1938), p. 2.

5. Mischa Titiev, *Old Oraibi: A Study of the Hopi Indians of Third Mesa*. Papers of the Peabody Museum of American Archeology and Ethnology. Harvard University, vol. 22 no. 1, p. 129.

Chapter 8. Western Great Lakes (Anishinabes): Mandamin

1. Robert E. Ritzenthaler, and Pat Ritzenthaler, *The Woodland Indians of the Western Great Lakes*. (Garden City, N. Y.: The Natural History Press, 1970), p. 12.

2. Corn and Indians of the Northeast: <http://www.tuscaroras.corn/pages/cornEX.html> (June 3, 2000).

3. Basil Johnston, *Ojibway Heritage*. (Lincoln: University of Nebraska Press, 1976), pp. 34–38.

4. Ibid., p. 7.

5. Edmund Jefferson Danziger Jr., *The Chippewas of Lake Superior*. (Norman: The University of Oklahoma Press, 1979), p. 20.

6. Joseph Campbell, *Historical Atlas of World Mythology. Vol. I: The Way of the Animal Powers: Part 2: Mythologies of the Great Hunt*. (New York: Harper & Row, 1988), p. 210.

Chapter 9. Eastern Woodlands (Micmacs): Glooscap the Teacher

1. Bruce G. Trigger, ed., *Handbook of the North American Indians*, vol. 15 (Washington, D.C.: Smithsonian Institution, 1978), p. 111.

2. Stith Thompson, *Tales of the North American Indians* (Bloomington: Indiana University Press, 1966), pp. 5–8.

3. *The Encyclopedia Americana*, vol. 21. (New York: Americana Corporation, 1968), p. 243a.

4. Lewis Spence, *The Myths of the North American Indians* (New York: Dover Publications, Inc., 1989), p. 141.

5. Dean B. Bennett, *Maine Dirigo "I Lead"* (Camden, Maine: Down East Books, 1980), p. 41.

◆× FURTHER READING ×◆

Ballard, Arthur C. *Mythology of Southern Puget Sound*. Seattle: University of Washington Press, 1929.

Barnouw, Victor. *Chippewa Myths & Tales and Their Relation to Chippewa Life*. Madison: The University of Wisconsin Press, 1977.

Bierhorst, John, *The Mythology of North America*. New York: William Morrow, 1985.

Boas, Franz. *Race, Language and Culture*. Chicago: The University of Chicago Press, 1982.

Bruchac, Joseph. *Keepers of the Earth*. Golden, Col.: Fulcrum, Inc., 1988.

Clark, Ella. E. *Indian Legends from the Northern Rockies*. Norman: University of Oklahoma Press, 1966.

Erdoes, Richard and Alfonso Ortiz, eds. *American Indian Myths and Legends*. New York: Pantheon Books, 1984.

Grinnell, George Bird. *By Cheyenne Campfires*. Lincoln: University of Nebraska Press, 1971.

———. *Blackfoot Lodge Tales*. Williamstown, Mass.: Corner House Publications, 1972.

Hudson, Charles. *The Southeastern Indians*. Knoxville: The University of Tennessee Press, 1976.

Johnston, Basil. *Ojibway Heritage*. Lincoln: University of Nebraska Press, 1976.

Keeper, Berry. *The Old Ones Told Me: American Indian Stories for Children*. Portland, Ore.: Binford & Mort, 1989.

Kroeber, A. L. *Handbook of the Indians of California*. New York: Dover Publications, Inc., 1976.

Kroeber, Theodora. *The Inland Whale*. Berkeley: University of California Press, 1959.

McHugh, Tom. *The Time of the Buffalo*. Lincoln: University of Nebraska Press, 1972.

Mooney, James. *History, Myths, and Sacred Formulas of the Cherokees*. Asheville, N. C.: Historical Images, 1992.

Nashone. *Grandmother Stories of the Northwest*. Newcastle, Calif.: Sierra Oaks Publishing Company, 1988.

Penny, Grace Jackson. *Tales of the Cheyennes*. Boston: Houghton Mifflin Co., 1953.

Sevillano, Mando. *The Hopi Way. Tales from a Vanishing Culture*. Flagstaff, Ariz.: Northland Press, 1986.

Shipley, William. *The Maidu Indian Myths and Stories of Hanc'ibyjim*. Berkeley, Calif.: Heyday Books, 1991.

Smith-Trafzer, Lee Ann, and Clifford E. Trafzer. *Creation of a California Tribe*. Sacramento, Calif.: Sierra Oaks Publishing Company, 1988.

Spence, Lewis. *The Myths of the North American Indians*. New York: Dover Publications, 1989.

Taylor, Colin F. *Native American Myths and Legends*. New York: Southmark Publishers, Inc., 1994.

Thompson, Stith. *Tales of the North American Indians*. Bloomington: Indiana University Press, 1966.

INTERNET ADDRESSES

Tribal names and their meanings:

http://members.tripod.com/~PHILKON/names.html

Tribal sites:

Northwest—Tsimshians

http://www.geocities.com/SoHo/Museum/4786/ P136-139.htm

Coast Plateau—Salish

http://maltwood.finearts.uvic.ca/nwcp/coastsal/intro.html

California—Maidu

http://www.778.com/maidu.html

Southeast—Cherokees

http://falcon.jmu.edu/~ramseyil/cherokees.htm

http://falcon.jmu.edu/~ramseyil/vaindianscherokee.htm

Northern Plains—Blackfeet

http://www.blackfoot.org/

Southern Plains—Cheyennes

http://www.geocities.com/Athens/Forum/3807/features/
cheyenne.html

Southwest—Hopi

http://www.uapress.arizona.edu/catalogs/native/hopi.htm

http://www.insects.org/ced4/dance.html

Western Great Lakes—Anishinabe

http://www.edwards1.com/rose/native/history.html

Eastern Woodlands—Micmacs

http://www.dickshovel.com/mic.html

http://www.mun.ca/rels/native/micmac/micmac1.html

INDEX

A

Abenaki, 109
Alaska, 8, 12, 25
Algonquian, 98, 105, 118
Anishinabes, 98, 101, 104, 105.
    See also Chippewa and
    Ojibway
antelope, 37, 73, 75, 99
Appalachian Mountains, 50
Arizona, 85
arctic, 23
Astor, John Jacob, 83

B

bears, 50, 75, 108
beavers, 108, 109
Bennett, Dean B., 118
Bierhorst, John, 35, 59
birds, 30, 32, 50, 53, 64, 67, 75.
    See also Raven
    Bluejay, 30, 31, 34, 53, 54
    Buzzard, 9, 50, 51, 53–55, 57,
        58
    Crow, 54
    ducks, 32
    Hawk, 40, 54
    Magpie, 54, 64, 67, 69, 70
    Owl, 53, 55
    sandpipers, 32
    Woodpecker, 30–32, 34
Blackfeet, 8, 9, 61–63, 69–71
Boas, Franz, 23, 35
Buffalo, 8, 61–66, 69–71, 73, 75,
    77, 78
    dance, 9, 62, 69, 70
buffalo-skin, 77, 79, 81
butterflies, 9, 40–46, 48

C

California, 8, 12, 37, 39, 48
camass bulbs, 25–28
Campbell, Joseph, 23, 71, 106
Canada, 8, 12, 61, 106, 108

British Columbia, 8, 12
canoes, 12, 20, 21, 32, 98, 109,
    111, 115
Cherokees, 9, 50, 55–59
Cheyennes, 8, 10, 72–83
Chippewa, 98, 106
Clark, William, 25
Coast Salish, 8, 9, 25. *See also*
    Salish
Columbia River, 25, 83
corn, 10, 50, 88, 90, 98, 104–106
    corncobs, 88, 90, 93
corral, 61
cradleboard, 29, 30, 39, 40, 41, 42
crawfish, 55, 57

D

Danziger, Edmund Jefferson Jr.,
    106
deer, 35, 37, 50, 54, 73, 75, 92, 93,
    99, 100, 110
Dockstader, Frederick J., 95

E

Earle, Edwin, 95
elk, 37, 50, 73, 75, 92, 93, 99, 108,
    110, 116

F

fish, 14, 20, 22, 35, 37, 50, 56, 57,
    99, 108, 109, 110, 111, 116.
    See also salmon
frogs, 14, 18, 20, 21

G

Gaspe Peninsula, 108
Great Lakes, 73
    western, 98
Great Plains, 8, 61, 73, 82. *See
    also* plains
Gulf of St. Lawrence, 108

H

Hoebel, E. Adamson, 83

Hopi, 9, 85–87, 92–96
Hudson, Charles, 58

I

Irving, Washington, 83

J

Johnston, Basil, 106

K

Kachinas, 9, 85, 86, 87, 93–96
Kennard, Edward A., 95
Kroeber, A. L., 48
Kroeber, Theodora, 48

L

Lenape, 5
Lewis, Meriwether, 25

M

Maidu, 37, 38, 48
Maliseet-Passamaquoddy, 109
McHugh, Tom, 71
Mexico, 25
Micmacs, 10, 108–111, 114–117
Minnesota, 83
Mississippi River, 8
Mojave Desert, 25
Montana, 61
moon, 9, 26, 32, 35, 58
Mooney, James, 58
Moyers, Bill, 71

N

Nass River, 12, 18
North Carolina, 58
North Dakota, 73
northeast, 110, 114, 116, 118
northwest, 11, 13,
    Coast, 8, 12, 31, 35

O

Ojibway, 98, 106

P

Pacific Coast, 23, 25, 31, 35
Pacific Northwest, 8, 12, 23
Pacific Ocean, 31
Pandora, 109, 117
pis'kun, 61, 62

plains, 10, 23, 82. *See also* Great
    Plains
    northern, 9, 61
    southern, 10, 74, 81, 82
potlatch, 12
Puget Sound, 25

R

rabbits, 90–93
Raven, 8, 9, 12–14, 18, 20–23,
    30–34, 53
Rocky Mountains, 8, 74

S

sagamore, 108
Salish, 25. *See also* Coast Salish
salmon, 8, 9, 12, 25, 30, 39, 108,
    111
    dog salmon, 25, 30–34
shellfish, 37, 108
Sierra Nevada Mountains, 25
Skeena River, 12
solstice: winter 10, 85, 86, 93, 94
South Dakota, 73
southeast, 58, 59
southwest, 9, 96
Spence, Lewis, 118
sun, 30, 32, 50, 54, 55, 57, 58, 74,
    98, 105

T

Texas, 8
tipis, 61, 63, 75, 77–80
Titiev, Mischa, 96
Tlingits, 8, 12
totem pole, 12, 22
travois, 73
trees, 29, 37, 50, 54, 55, 57, 101,
    114
trickster, 9, 10, 20, 22, 23, 109
    trickster-transformer, 109, 116
Tsimshians, 8, 9, 12, 22, 23

W

Wabanakis, 118
Washington State, 25
wigwams, 98, 100, 101, 108, 113,
    115, 116